NEW TESTAMENT GREECE AND ROME

TEACHERS GUIDE

*With tremendous gratitude
we wish to acknowledge
and express our appreciation
to those who assisted in the
making of this manual:*

Ned Bustard
Christi McCullars
Shea Foster
Emily Fischer
and Aaron Larsen

Veritas Press

Dear Friends,

We hope this guide will be helpful as you study the New Testament, Greece, and Rome this year. You are about to take a journey through the past where you can see God's providence, judgement, and provision for His people on a daily basis. This study should help build an understanding of the world into which Christ was born, the tremendous suffering our Lord bore for our sins and the persecution our Christian forefathers experienced. And then we finally see a victory of sorts for Christianity with the Edict of Milan. God was faithful to His people through the years just as He is today. What a joy it is for young children to come to realize God's faithfulness as they learn from the past.

There are 32 events/people featured in the cards in this series. That is approximately one per week. A few of the cards have extra projects which may spread into the following week. The projects are only suggestions, so use your imagination and have fun with your group. You will note that the projects vary to appeal to different ages. You may choose the ones you think are appropriate for your student(s). We recommend singing the song daily for the first several weeks, after that three times a week is usually enough. Remember, the reason for the song is to help memorize the chronology of the events. It is also good to have the children recite events, in proper order, rather that singing it after the song has been memorized. A sample school week might be planned as follows:

MONDAY: Sing the song (you may want to have a student come to the front of the room and hold up the flashcards in order as the class sings). Present the new card. Read what it says on the back and discuss it. Allow different students to read it out loud if you can. Then allow the students to answer questions on the worksheet. The questions are based on information on the cards.

TUESDAY: Sing the song. Orally review questions from this card's worksheet and from previous events. Obviously you cannot review every questions every day, so do a sampling. Assign different children different sources from the resource list on the card and allow them to look up the information and share it with the class.

WEDNESDAY: Sing the song. Orally review questions from the worksheet. Do one of the projects.

THURSDAY: Sing the song. Orally review from this week and previous weeks. Discuss how this card relates to those before it. Do another project, if there is one.

FRIDAY: Give test. Use remaining time for class instruction and drill. If you have already studied the Old Testament/Ancient Egypt series we strongly encourage review and testing of that series. Appendix 1 is provided for testing the student(s) on four different cards each week.

Having fun makes it easy to learn. Using the cards for games is one way. Ask the children to shuffle them and then see who can get their cards in order the fastest. Or have four to six students mix up their cards and then play Go Fish. This allows them to get familiar with the titles. Or you can get in a large room and see who can make their own timeline the fastest. A good way to drill questions in a classroom is to divide the children into two teams and ask questions in order. Teams receive a point for each right answer.

We have found one of the best ways to file the cards is to laminate them, punch a hole in the top right corner, and keep them on a large ring. The children can add the newest card and also have the previous cards handy. Another idea is to laminate them, put a Velcro strip on the card and on the wall, and start a timeline that children can put up and take down over and over again. An extra set of cards mounted at the end of the room for a reference timeline is a good idea too.

In order to encourage children to read historical fiction related to classroom work, we suggest a book chart to show points earned for each book read by each student. After receiving a certain number of points we allow the child to have a special lunch with their teacher. You could have a mom bring in a special lunch or allow the winners to go out.

Each worksheet, test, or writing assignment should receive three grades, one each for Content, Grammar and Linguistics (Spelling).

GRADING: A grading scale you may find helpful is to count ten points for essay questions, five points for one sentence answers and two points for fill in the blank answers. The percentile grade will then be the total number of points achieved divided by the total number of points possible.

GRAMMAR: The child should answer the questions in a complete sentence in which they first restate the question. For example: What is the Scripture reference for Creation? The Scripture reference for Creation is Genesis 1-2. This grade should be applied to an application grade in grammar, but should not affect history content grades. We suggest application at twenty percent of the overall grade.

LINGUISTICS: The children should spell all words correctly. You should deduct for misspelled words once the rule for spelling a particular word has been mastered. For example: i before e except after c. Once this has been covered a child's grade would be reduced if they spelled receive as receive. If they are using a history card to do their worksheet they should be taught that those words to be transcribed directly from the card should be spelled correctly. This grade would be applied towards a linguistics application grade. Again we suggest twenty percent, but not to affect their history grade.

When you look at the tests you will see that there are not the same number of questions on each test or worksheet. We assign five points per question, with the listings of the chronology receiving two points per item listed. Partial credit may be counted because the questions are essay and they may have portions correct. Some students may ask why they are receiving three grades on each paper. We believe that it is important for a student to realize that grammar and linguistics matter in history class as well as in grammar class. All three contribute to help make students understood by others, and are thus intertwined.

Finally we welcome your feedback and comments. We hope that his resource will enrich the education of those children entrusted to you, and will help them understand the comprehensive responsibility that God requires of them.

Sincerely,

Marlin and Laurie Detweiler
Veritas Press
September 15, 1998

NEW TESTAMENT, GREECE, AND ROME
Teachers Guide

TABLE OF CONTENTS

MINOAN CULTURE
Worksheet

1. What are the approximate dates of the Minoan Culture?

   _____

   _____

2. What was the first European civilization? Where did it develop?

   _____

   _____

3. Who was King Minos?

   _____

   _____

4. Where did the Minoans choose to build their towns?

   _____

   _____

5. How did the Minoans travel? What is the primary reason they traveled so much?

   _____

   _____

6. Where did they build their largest palace?

   _____

   _____

   _____

   _____

7. Why is it thought the Minoans believed in life after death?

_____

_____

8. What alphabet did the Minoans develop?

_____

_____

9. How is their culture best described?

_____

_____

10. How is it thought the Minoan civilization ended?

_____

_____

_____

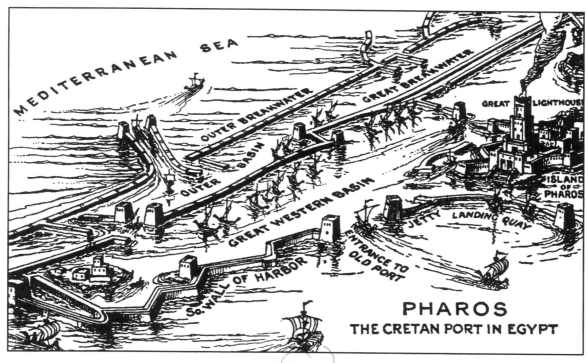

PHAROS
THE CRETAN PORT IN EGYPT

MINOAN CULTURE
Project
Frescos

Much of what we have learned about the Minoans has come from frescos painted on palace walls. Frescos are paints done on wet plaster. The paint absorbs into the plaster as the plaster dries and through the years does not fade much. In particular, the frescos at Knossos have given archaeologists valuable information about the Minoan culture. They have learned much about the Minoan dress and life events from these paintings.

Minoan artwork is not still, but full of motion. When looking at the paintings, you feel as if they are moving. The people appear to be very graceful and full of life. Many times animals were painted in the frescos with the people.

On the following page you will find instructions for making your own fresco.

MINOAN CULTURE
Project, Page 2

Materials

Plaster of Paris

Styrofoam vegetable trays (can usually be obtained from grocery stores)

pencil

water color paints and brush

vegetable oil

Instructions

Mix Plaster of Paris according to instructions on package.
Rub or spray tray with vegetable oil.
Pour plaster into tray to make it 3/4 full. Allow to dry.
With examples from card and other available resources draw your own typical
  but unique fresco.
Paint the scene with water colors.

MINOAN CULTURE
Project 2

Many frescos were done about bull-leaping. There may be a good reason for this. The bull may have become sacred to the people. We do know of a famous Greek myth about the Minotaur.

The Minotaur

There were almost as many stories of heroes as of gods. The heroes were men who had done some deed of great bravery. They were usually the sons of a god or goddess and a human being. Almost every Greek city had its hero. The favorite of Athens, for instance was Theseus; and every Athenian child knew the story of his wonderful exploits, and could tell of the old days when every year Athens had to send seven brave youths and seven fair maidens to Crete to be devoured by the Minotaur, a horrible creature with the body of a man and the head of a bull. At last, Theseus, the king's son, insisted upon being one of the seven youths; and he left Athens in the ship with black sails that carried terrified young people to their awful fate. Now Theseus had no idea of being eaten by the Minotaur or any other monster, if sturdy fighting could prevent it. He was determined to kill the beast and save his friends or perish. So when the vessel reached Crete and the youths and maidens were brought before the king, he stood out in front of them and said: "King Minos, I demand the privilege of meeting the Minotaur first. I am a prince, and it is my right to be the leader of my people." King Minos smiled disagreeably and said: "Go first if you will, and I will see to it that your people follow you; depend upon that."

Theseus was a brave young fighter, and certainly he would never have run away from the monster; but whether he would have been able to kill it without any help is another question. In some way, however, he and the king's beautiful daughter Ariadne had met, and they had fallen in love with each other. Luckily for him, Ariadne knew where to find a sword that in the hands of a valiant man would cut off the Minotaur's ugly head. There was yet another danger to meet that was even more alarming than an encounter with a monster, and that was the labyrinth which was the home of the Minotaur (Some say this labyrinth may have been based on the palace in Knossos because it would have seemed like a maze with all its rooms and corridors.) It had been made by a most skillful workman named Daedalus, and was so cunningly contrived, with its mazes and windings and turns and twists, that no one who was once within it could ever find his way out. Not even a magic weapon would be of service here; but Ariadne's own bright wits were better than any sword. "Hold fast one end of this silken cord," she said to Theseus, "and I will hold the ball as it unwinds. Then when you turn to come back, wind the little cord, and it will lead you straight to me." It all came about as she had said. Theseus killed the monster, then he followed the silken clue till it brought him again to Ariadne. He and the princess and the Athenian youths and maidens sailed away quickly for Athens; and never again did the Athenians pay such a terrible tribute.

Although myths like this are obviously not true. They impacted the Greek society greatly. As Christians we measure all we hear and see by the Word of God.

Theseus and the Minotaur

MINOAN CULTURE
Test

1. What was the first European civilization? Where did it develop?

   _____

   _____

2. What title did the Greeks use for their king that was similar to the Egyptian term "Pharaoh?"

   _____

   _____

3. Where did the Minoans build their towns? Why?

   _____

   _____

4. How did the Minoans travel? For what reason did they travel?

   _____

   _____

5. Where was the largest Minoan built palace?

   _____

   _____

6. Why is it assumed that the Minoans believed in life after death?

   _____

   _____

7. What is the name of the early Greek alphabet developed by the Minoans?

   _____

   _____

8. What typified the lifestyle of the Minoans?

   _____

   _____

9. What is believed to have caused the end of the Minoan culture?

_____

_____

10. What are the approximate dates of the Minoan culture?

_____

_____

MYCENAEN CULTURE
Worksheet

1. What is the approximate date of the Mycenaen Culture?

   _____

   _____

2. Of what lands did the warring Mycenaens gain control by 1450 BC?

   _____

   _____

3. From what did the Mycenaen civilization receive it's name?

   _____

   _____

4. How do we know that the Mycenaens settled the Peloponessus?

   _____

   _____

5. What was the nature of the Mycenaen people?

   _____

   _____

MYCENAEN CULTURE
Worksheet, Page 2

6. What was a citadel or acropolis? How did the Mycenaens use them?
   Describe a particular one.

   _____

   _____

   _____

   _____

7. Name the typical items exported by the Mycenaens. How do we know
   they exported these things?

   _____

   _____

   _____

8. What was the primary way the Mycenaens supported their economy?

   _____

   _____

9. How did the Mycenaen Culture end?

   _____

   _____

   _____

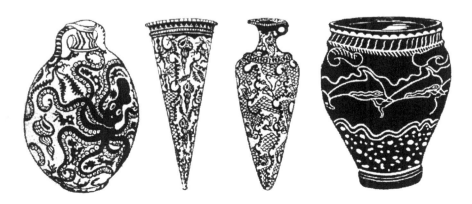

MYCENAEN CULTURE
Project
Mycenaen Pottery

The palace was the center of economic life. Crops were kept in store rooms to use or be exported. Pottery and other items to be exported were produced by skilled artisans or craftsman who worked for the king. The craftsman had workshops on the citadel (or acropolis) where they produced pottery including pots, jars, and statues to be used by the king and his family, exported, or as payment to other craftsman and soldiers.

MYCENAEN CULTURE
Project, Page 2

Mycenaen Pottery

Materials

air-drying clay

bowl of water

clay tools or a pencil

tempera paint

Instructions

Take a lump of clay about the size of a
    golf ball, roll it into a sphere and then
    flatten to a circle that is
    approximately 3/8" thick.

Take a second lump of clay the same size
    as the first and roll it into a cylinder
    about 3/8" thick.

Score the flat circle with tools or pencil
    by making 1" score lines near the edge
    perpendicular to it. (See "A")

Take the cylinder and wrap it around the
    edge of the circle to build the first
    layer on top of the pot base.

Repeat until desired height is achieved.
    (See "B")

Wet hands and smooth walls of pot.
    (See "C")

Shape as desired and allow to dry.

Paint the pot after it is dry. (Use pictures
    from resources for ideas as to
    colors and designs.)

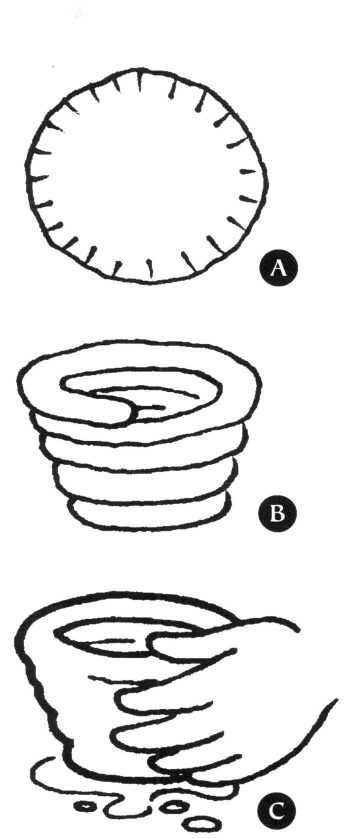

MYCENAEN CULTURE
Test

1. What are the approximate dates of the Mycenaen Culture?

   _____

   _____

2. From what did the civilization receive its name?

   _____

   _____

3. What was found at Athens and Thebes that has aided our understanding of the Mycenaens?

   _____

   _____

4. Describe what typified the Mycenaen's lifestyle.

   _____

   _____

5. Describe the features of a citadel (or acropolis).

   _____

   _____

6. What were the occupations and careers of the Mycenaens?

   _____

   _____

7. How do we know the Mycenaens were skilled artisans?

   _____

   _____

8. What caused the end of the Mycenaen civilization?

   _____

   _____

TROJAN WAR
Worksheet

1. Did the Trojan War actually ever occur?

   _____

   _____

2. What is the approximate date of the war which the Trojan War resembles?

   _____

   _____

3. Describe and name the person who wrote the Iliad? What is it about?

   _____

   _____

   _____

4. What group of people joined together to defeat the Trojans?

   _____

   _____

5. How did the Greeks get inside Troy?

   _____

   _____

   _____

6. How was the city of Troy destroyed?

TROJAN WAR
Project 2

Trojan Horse Model
Supplies
Beige or white heavy construction paper
markers
tempera paint
glue
scissors
twine

Instructions
1. Photocopy onto beige or white construction paper the image of the horse and warriors.
2. Cut out the images.
3. Paint the horse brown with tempera paint. Detail with black as necessary.
4. Cut the entrance/exit in the side of the horse.
5. Color the warriors with markers.
6. Attach twine to the entrance/exit of the horse side.
7. Attach the warriors to the twine so as to have them "climbing out of the horse".

You may want to build a larger version from refrigerator boxes and have the children attack another class from the inside of it.

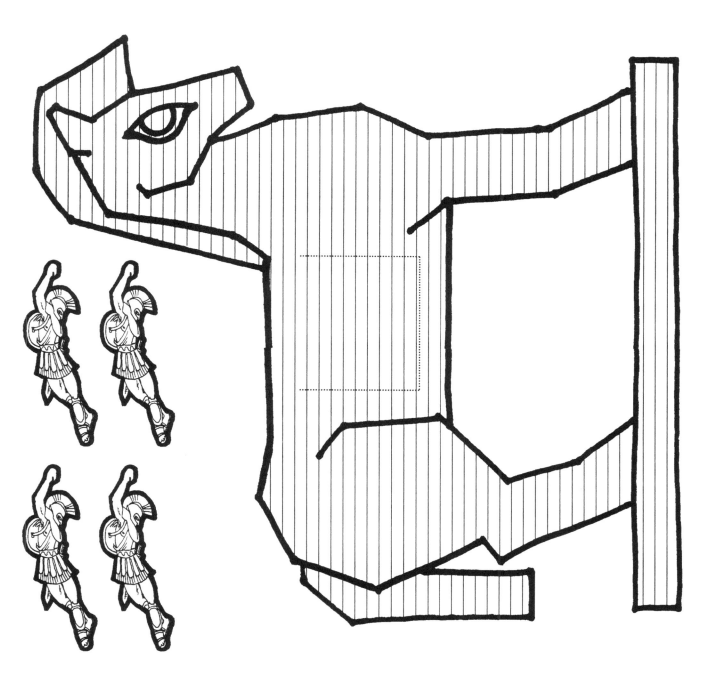

TROJAN WAR
Project 2—Literature Unit

The Trojan Horse, How the Greeks Won the War

CHAPTER ONE

The Wall

1. On the back draw a picture of the city of Troy.

2. In what modern country was Troy located?

_____

_____

3. What surrounded Troy?

_____

_____

4. Give two reasons why no one could climb over the wall.

_____

_____

5. What was the only way to enter Troy?

_____

_____

6. Who was the King of Troy? Why was he not content?

_____

_____

7. Why did the Greeks pay a toll to pass through the channel connecting the Aegean and Black Seas?

_____

_____

_____

TROJAN WAR
Project 2, Page 2—Literature Unit

CHAPTER TWO — *Just tell the story in your own words* —

War

1. What was the name of King Menelaus' wife? What happened to her?

_____

_____

2. Who was King Menelaus' brother? What message did he receive?

_____

_____

3. Why did the Greeks go to war?

_____

_____

4. Who was Athena? Why did both the Greeks and Trojans bring her a gift?

_____

_____

_____

5. Who won the first battle? Who won the battles in the following years?

_____

_____

6. What was the only way Odysseus believed the Greeks could defeat Troy?

_____

_____

_____

_____

TROJAN WAR
Project 2, Page 3—Literature Unit

Illustrate building the the Trojan Horse and how it was used.

TROJAN WAR
Project 2, Page 4—Literature Unit

CHAPTER FOUR

Doom is Near!

1. What did King Priam say the Trojans should do to the wooden horse?

_____

_____

_____

_____

_____

2. When Sinon the Greek is found what did he tell the Trojans about the horse?

_____

_____

_____

_____

_____

3. Eventually what did the Trojans do with the wooden horse?

_____

_____

_____

_____

_____

_____

Trojan War
Project 2, Page 5—Literature Unit

CHAPTER FIVE

The Fall

Write a paragraph describing what happened to the city of Troy after darkness fell upon it.

_____

_____

_____

_____

_____

_____

_____

_____

_____

_____

_____

_____

_____

TROJAN WAR
Project 2, Page 6—Literature Unit

CHAPTER SIX

Discovery

1. Who wrote about the Trojan War?

2. What was the name of the poem he wrote about the Trojan War?

   What Greek literature is older than this poem?

3. What famous archaeologist discovered the ruins of Troy?

4. What did the archaeologist find? What notable items did he not find?

TROJAN WAR
Test

1. What is the approximate date the Trojan War supposedly occurred?

   _____

   _____

2. Who wrote the poem about the Trojan War? What was it called?

   _____

   _____

3. Describe the legend of the Trojan War.

   _____

   _____

   _____

   _____

   _____

   _____

4. How did the Greeks defeat the Trojans?

   _____

   _____

   _____

   _____

   _____

   _____

   _____

   _____

Review

1. What was the first European civilization?

   _____

   _____

2. What is a Greek term similar to the Egyptian term "Pharaoh?"

   _____

   _____

3. What is the name of the alphabet developed by the Minoans?

   _____

   _____

4. Describe Mycenean culture.

   _____

   _____

   _____

   _____

5. What caused the end of Mycenean civilization?

   _____

   _____

   _____

   _____

   _____

   _____

   _____

PHOENICIAN CIVILIZATION AND THE ALPHABET
Worksheet

1. What were the approximate dates of the Phoenicians Civilization?

   _____

   _____

2. Where did the Phoenicians live? What were they known as in the Bible?

   _____

   _____

   _____

3. How did the name "Phoenicians" develop?

   _____

   _____

4. What were the predominant occupations of the Phoenicians?

   _____

   _____

5. Why were they known as the greatest seafarers of the ancient world?

   _____

   _____

6. What was the Phoenicians most important contribution to civilization?

   _____

   _____

7. How many consonants did their
   alphabet have? How many vowels?

   _____

   _____

   _____

PHŒNICIAN CIVILIZATION AND THE ALPHABET
Project

Greeting Card

PHŒNICIAN	LATER GREEK	LATIN
		A
		B
		C G
		D
		E
		F V
		(Z)
		H
		(TH, PH)
		I
		K, KH
		L
		M
		N
		X
		O
		P
		(S)
		Q
		R
		S
		T

Reproduce the following page to make a card for your parents that uses the Phoenician alphabet. Color the fresco and then in the space provided under the image, translate the words below using the Phoenician alphabet.

Then write a personal note of thanks using *our* alphabet on the inside that expresses your gratitude for the education they are giving you.

"Mom and Dad, I love you and by the way..."

Cover:
FLORAL FRESCO FROM THE
PALACE OF KNOSSOS

Veritas Press
CARDS

Fine Greeting Cards Since the Dawn of Time

g04-3

PHOENICIAN CIVILIZATION AND THE ALPHABET
Project 2

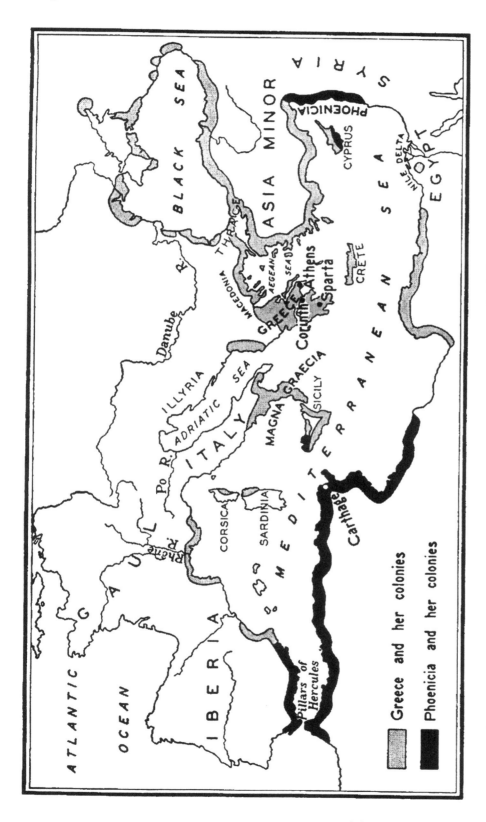

The Phoenicians settled along the coast of present day Lebanon. They used the sea and their great ships to make a living by trading along the Mediterranean coastline. They established colonies to assist in their trading at many points on the coast.

Discuss the geographic relationship of Egypt, Crete, and Greece with the Phoenician trade routes.

PHOENICIAN CIVILIZATION AND THE ALPHABET
Test

1. What is the approximate date of the Phoenician Civilization?

   _____

   _____

2. What is the relationship between the Canaanites and the Phoenicians?

   _____

   _____

3. From what did the Phoenicians receive their name?

   _____

   _____

4. What was the Phoenicians most important contribution to civilization?

   _____

   _____

   _____

5. What were the predominant occupations for the Phoenician people?

   _____

   _____

6. What is the translation of the Greek word "phoinos?"

   _____

   _____

   _____

7. How many letters were in the Phoenician alphabet? How many vowels did this include?

   _____

   _____

Review

1. What was the first European civilization?

   _____

   _____

2. What were some of the items produced by the skilled artisans of Mycenae?

   _____

   _____

   _____

3. Who popularized the story of the Trojan War?

   What was the name of the book in which he wrote about it?

   _____

   _____

   _____

4. Why is it thought the Minoans believed in life after death?

   _____

   _____

   _____

5. Describe the Mycenaen culture.

   _____

   _____

   _____

   _____

   _____

   _____

ISRAEL DIVIDES INTO TWO KINGDOMS
Worksheet

1. What is the approximate date that Israel divided into Two Kingdoms?

   _____

   _____

2. What was the reason Israel was divided?

   _____

   _____

3. Where is this event recorded in Scripture?

   _____

   _____

4. Who was king when Israel was divided into two kingdoms?

   Why did it not happen during Solomon's reign?

   _____

   _____

   _____

5. Who was Jeroboam?

   _____

   _____

   _____

6. Who was Ahijah?

   _____

   _____

7. Who was Rehoboam?

   _____

   _____

   _____

ISRAEL DIVIDES INTO TWO KINGDOMS
Project

Read 1 Kings 11. Using complete sentences, write a paragraph describing the Biblical meaning in the picture.

_____

_____

_____

_____

_____

_____

_____

_____

_____

_____

ISRAEL DIVIDES INTO TWO KINGDOMS
Project 2

Mapping the Kingdoms

Color the Kingdom of Judah yellow, the Kingdom of Israel orange, Phoenicia purple, Mediterranean Sea blue, and Babylonia pink.

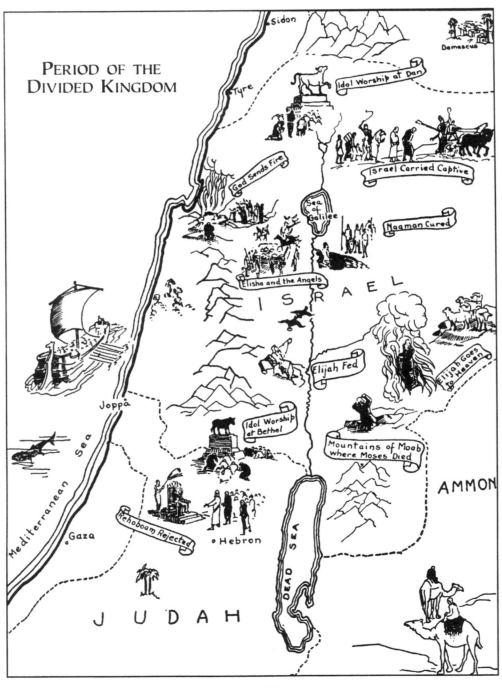

ISRAEL DIVIDES INTO TWO KINGDOMS
Test

1. What is the Scripture reference for Israel Divides into Two Kingdoms?

   _____

   _____

2. Approximately when was Israel divided?

   _____

   _____

3. Why was Israel divided?

   _____

   _____

4. Who was king when Israel was divided? Who became ruler of each of the kingdoms?

   _____

   _____

   _____

5. What prophet appeared to Jeroboam? What did he tell him?

   _____

   _____

   _____

6. What did Jeroboam do before ruling the divided kingdom?

   _____

   _____

   _____

7. Why did God not split the kingdom during Solomon's reign?

   _____

   _____

   _____

ISRAEL DIVIDES INTO TWO KINGDOMS
Test, Page 2

Review

1. Where did the Minoans build their towns? Why?

_____

_____

2. What is a citadel?

_____

_____

3. How did the Minoans support their economy?

_____

_____

4. What trick did the Greeks use to defeat the Trojans as recorded in The Iliad?

_____

_____

5. What were the Phoenicians known as in Scripture?

_____

_____

HOMER AND GREEK MYTHOLOGY
Worksheet

1. When is it believed that Homer lived?

   _____

   _____

2. What was Homer's profession?

   _____

   _____

3. What were Homer's most famous stories?

   _____

   _____

4. What physical problem did Homer have?

   _____

   _____

5. How did the Greeks explain the world around them during Homer's day?

   _____

   _____

6. Name three Greek gods.

   _____

   _____

7. Describe the similarities and differences
   between the Greek gods and man.

   _____

   _____

   _____

   _____

HOMER AND GREEK MYTHOLOGY
Project

Homer, the Great Storyteller

A long, long time ago—perhaps three thousand years or more--there was a man named Homer. No one knows much about him; but there are legends that he was born on the island of Chios and that he was blind. He wandered about the land, homeless, but was welcomed wherever he chose to go, because he was a poet (then known as a bard). He once described how a blind poet was treated at a great banquet, and probably that is the way in which people treated him. He said that when the feast was ready, a page was sent to lead in the honored guest. A silver-studded chair was brought forward for him and set against a pillar. On the pillar the page hung his harp, so near him that he could touch it if he wished. A little table was placed before him, and on it was put a tray spread with food and wine. When the feasting was at an end, he sang a glorious song of the mighty deeds of men. The Greeks liked to hear stories just as well as the people of today, and they shouted with delight. Then they all went out to the racecourse, the page leading the blind singer carefully along the way. There were races and wrestling matches and boxing and throwing of the discus. After this, the poet took his harp and stepped to the center of the circle. The young men gathered around him eagerly, and he chanted a story of Ares, the war god, and Aphrodite, goddess of beauty and love.

Illustrate Homer as a bard in the frame below.

HOMER AND GREEK MYTHOLOGY
Project 2—Literature Unit

D'Aulaires' Book of Greek Myths

READ IN OLDEN TIMES (PAGE 9)

1. How did the Greeks gods originate?

   _____

   _____

2. Describe the Greek gods.

   _____

   _____

   _____

3. Where did the Greek gods live?

   _____

   _____

4. What did the Greek gods look like when visiting earth?

   _____

   _____

5. Who did the Greeks believe began all of life?

   _____

   _____

6. What do we, as Christians, know about the Greek's beliefs?

   _____

   _____

   _____

   _____

   _____

HOMER AND GREEK MYTHOLOGY
Project 2, Page 2—Literature Unit

D'Aulaires' Book of Greek Myths

READ GAEA, MOTHER EARTH (PAGE 10)

Write a paragraph on the lines below explaining the Greeks' creation story that was their explanation of how the world began.

_____

_____

_____

_____

_____

_____

_____

_____

_____

_____

_____

_____

_____

_____

_____

_____

_____

_____

_____

_____

HOMER AND GREEK MYTHOLOGY
Project 2, Page 3—Literature Unit

D'Aulaires' Book of Greek Myths

READ THE TITANS (PAGES 12 - 15)

1. What name was given to the group of Mother Earth's first children. List their names.

   _____

   _____

2. When Gaea gave birth again, Uranus was not proud.

   On the back draw a picture of these new children to show why he did not like them.

3. When Gaea gave birth once again Uranus was disgusted. What did he do?

   _____

   _____

4. What did Mother Earth ask her sons, the Titans, to do to their father?

   _____

   _____

5. On the back draw a picture of the fight between Uranus and Cronus.

   _____

   _____

6. Who was Mother Earth's second husband?

   _____

   _____

   _____

   _____

   _____

HOMER AND GREEK MYTHOLOGY
Project 2, Page 4—Literature Unit

D'Aulaires' Book of Greek Myths

7. Who was now lord of the universe? Why did Mother Earth become angry with him?

_____

_____

_____

_____

8. Why did Cronus swallow his children?

_____

_____

_____

9. Draw a picture of Cronus on the back.

10. Rhea, Cronus's wife, asked Mother Earth to help her save her sixth child.

    What was the child's name?   What did they do?

_____

_____

_____

_____

_____

_____

_____

_____

HOMER AND GREEK MYTHOLOGY
Project 2, Page 5—Literature Unit

D'Aulaires' Book of Greek Myths

READ ZEUS AND HIS FAMILY (PAGES 16 - 23)

1. Zeus was tended by gentle _____ and was nursed by the fairy

   _____ _____.

2. What did Zeus receive to eat?

   _____

   _____

3. What did Zeus make from the hide of the goat?

   _____

   _____

4. Who was Zeus's first wife? Of what was she the goddess?

   _____

   _____

5. What advice did Zeus's wife give him about overpowering his father?

   _____

   _____

   _____

6. Who tricked Cronus into eating a magic herb? What did eating it cause him to do?

   _____

   _____

   _____

7. Why did Cronus surrender his powers to Zeus?

   _____

   _____

   _____

D'Aulaires' Book of Greek Myths

8. Zeus was now the lord of the _____. He did not want to rule

   _____. He shared his powers with his _____ and _____.

   But, the _____ and their sons revolted. They refused to let themselves be

   ruled by the new _____. Only _____ and his brother _____

   left the Titans to join Zeus, for Prometheus could look into the _____,

   He knew that _____ would win.

9. Who did Zeus free to fight with him? What did they make for Zeus use to fight?

   _____

   _____

10. What did Zeus do to the Titans after he defeated them in what was a terrible battle?

    _____

    _____

11. Angry with Zeus for sending her sons, the _____ into the dark pit of

    _____, Mother Earth now brought forth two _____ _____

    and sent them against Zeus. Zeus fought a battle with them and sent

    _____ into the Mountain Aetna to be trapped forever.

12. What happened to Echidna, Typhon's hideous mate?

    _____

    _____

    _____

    _____

    _____

    _____

HOMER AND GREEK MYTHOLOGY
Project 2, Page 7—Literature Unit

D'Aulaires' Book of Greek Myths

ZEUS AND HIS FAMILY

Hera

1. Describe Hera's personality.

_____

_____

2. What did Zeus do to Io to protect her from Hera?

_____

_____

3. What was unusual about Argus, Hera's servant who was to watch over Io?

_____

_____

4. How did Hermes get past Argus?

_____

_____

5. From where do the eyes on a peacock come?

_____

_____

Hephaestus

1. Of what was Hephaestus the god?

_____

_____

HOMER AND GREEK MYTHOLOGY
Project 2, Page 8—Literature Unit

D'Aulaires' Book of Greek Myths

2. What did Hephaestus build to help him?

_____

_____

3. Who was Hephaestus' wife?

_____

_____

Aphrodite

1. What was unusual about Aphrodite's background?

_____

_____

2. Who was Aphrodite's son?

_____

_____

3. How did Aphrodite stay young and beautiful?

_____

_____

Ares

1. Describe Ares' personality.

_____

_____

_____

Homer and Greek Mythology
Project 2, Page 9—Literature Unit

D'Aulaires' Book of Greek Myths

2. What did Eris like to do?

_____

_____

3. How did Ares handle pain?

_____

_____

Athena

1. How was Athena born?

_____

_____

2. Why did Zeus swallow Metis?

_____

_____

3. What was Arachne's foolish boast?

_____

_____

4. Into what did Athena turn Arachne?

_____

_____

5. What was Athena's gift to Athens?

_____

_____

D'Aulaires' Book of Greek Myths

6. What did Athena do for Athens?

_____

_____

Poseidon

1. Of what was Poseidon the god?

_____

_____

2. Who was Poseidon's wife?

_____

_____

3. Who were the twins born on the island of Delos?

_____

_____

Apollo

1. In what did Apollo ride?

_____

_____

2. What did Python guard?

_____

_____

D'Aulaires' Book of Greek Myths

3. Who killed Python?

_____

_____

Artemis

1. Who was Artemis' twin brother?

_____

_____

2. What did Artemis request of Zeus?

_____

_____

3. Why did Artemis change Actaeon into a stag?

_____

_____

4. How was Actaeon killed?

_____

_____

5. What do Otus and Ephialtes do with Ares?

_____

_____

6. How were Otus and Ephialtes killed?

_____

_____

HOMER AND GREEK MYTHOLOGY
Project 2, Page 12—Literature Unit

D'Aulaires' Book of Greek Myths

7. What did the King of Chios do to Orion so Orion could not take his daughter?

_____

_____

8. How did Orion die?

_____

_____

9. What was done with Orion's image so he would not be forgotten?

_____

_____

Hermes

1. Whose cows did Hermes steal?

_____

_____

2. How did Hermes erase the tracks when he stole the cows?

_____

_____

3. What did Hermes give in return for the whole herd?

_____

_____

4. What three things did Zeus give to Hermes?

_____

_____

HOMER AND GREEK MYTHOLOGY
Project 2, Page 13—Literature Unit

D'Aulaires' Book of Greek Myths

Hades

1. Why was Hades called the Hospitable One?

_____

_____

2. What was the river that flowed around the underworld?

_____

_____

3. Who was the ferryman to the underworld?

_____

_____

4. What was Cerberus?

_____

_____

Persephone and Demeter

1. What did Demeter threaten she would do if she did not get her daughter back?

_____

_____

2. Why did Persephone have to go back to Hades?

_____

_____

3. What causes the seasons according to Greek mythology?

_____

_____

HOMER AND GREEK MYTHOLOGY
Project 2, Page 14—Literature Unit

D'Aulaires' Book of Greek Myths

Dionysus

1. How did Semele die?

_____

_____

2. What did Dionysus invent?

_____

_____

3. Into what did Dionysus change the sailors?

_____

_____

4. Who gave up her throne so Dionysus could have a throne?

_____

_____

MINOR GODS, NYMPHS, SATYRS, AND CENTAURS

Prometheus

1. What were Prometheus and Epimetheus given the task of creating?

_____

_____

2. What did Prometheus steal?

_____

_____

HOMER AND GREEK MYTHOLOGY
Project 2, Page 15—Literature Unit

D'Aulaires' Book of Greek Myths

3. What happened when men got fire?

_____

_____

4. Why did Zeus chose the offering of the scraps and entrails?

_____

_____

5. What was Prometheus' punishment for teaching humans to cheat the gods?

_____

_____

Pandora

1. Zeus had given Pandora insatiable _____ and then gave her a

_____ and warned her _____.

2. The moment she opened the _____, out swarmed _____.

3. Pandora clapped the lid on just in time to keep _____ inside. If it had gotten

out, the miseries would have _____.

Deucalion

1. What did Deucalion build?

_____

_____

2. How was Deucalion's race formed?

_____

_____

HOMER AND GREEK MYTHOLOGY
Project 2, Page 16—Literature Unit

D'Aulaires' Book of Greek Myths

Eos

1. Who was Eos?

_____

_____

2. What did Zeus grant Tithonus?

_____

_____

3. What happened to Tithonus since he did not ask for eternal youth?

_____

_____

Helios and Phaethon

1. What did Helios do?

_____

_____

2. What did Helios ride in at night?

_____

_____

3. For what did Phaethon wish?

_____

_____

_____

HOMER AND GREEK MYTHOLOGY
Project 2, Page 17—Literature Unit

D'Aulaires' Book of Greek Myths

4. What did Zeus have to do to save the earth from destruction?

_____

_____

Pan

1. What was unique about Pan's body?

_____

_____

Echo, Syrinx and the Wild and Vulgar Centaurs

1. What did Hera take away from Echo?

_____

_____

2. How did Daphne escape Apollo?

_____

_____

3. Draw a Centaur on the back.

Asclepius

1. At what was Asclepius particularly gifted?

_____

_____

2. How did Asclepius die?

_____

HOMER AND GREEK MYTHOLOGY
Project 2, Page 18—Literature Unit

D'Aulaires' Book of Greek Myths

Muses

1. How many Muses were there?

_____

_____

2. What did Mnemosyne teach her daughters?

_____

_____

3. What did Apollo teach the Muses?

_____

_____

Orpheus

1. What happened to Orpheus' wife on her wedding day?

_____

_____

2. Why did Orpheus go the underworld?

_____

_____

3. What happened to Orpheus when he looked back to see if Euridice was behind him?

_____

_____

_____

HOMER AND GREEK MYTHOLOGY
Project 2, Page 19—Literature Unit

D'Aulaires' Book of Greek Myths

MORTAL DESCENDANTS OF ZEUS

Danaus, Perseus, and the Gorgon

1. In each group of events number the sentences to show the order in which they occured.

_____ The 49 daughters killed their husbands.

_____ King Danaus fled in a ship so his brother's sons would not marry his daughters.

_____ Their was no heir to King Danaus' throne.

_____ Acrisius put Danae in a sealed chamber.

_____ Danae and Zeus had a son named Perseus.

_____ Danae and Perseus were put out to sea in a chest.

_____ Acrisius heard that Danae's son would kill him.

2. How did the following items help Perseus on his quest?

   a. eye of the Gray Sisters _____

   _____

   b. shield _____

   _____

   c. magic bag _____

   _____

3. What happened to Perseus and Andromeda when they died?

   _____

   _____

HOMER AND GREEK MYTHOLOGY
Project 2, Page 20—Literature Unit

D'Aulaires' Book of Greek Myths

Clever and Vainglorious Kings

Explain the pictures of the kings on the following pages.

1. Midas (p. 125) _____

_____

2. Sisyphus (p. 127) _____

_____

3. Bellerophon (p. 128) _____

_____

4. Melampus (p. 130) _____

_____

Heracles

1. Why did Heracles have to do the ten labors?

_____

_____

2. List the ten labors that Heracles had to do.

_____

_____

_____

_____

_____

_____

_____

_____

HOMER AND GREEK MYTHOLOGY
Project 2, Page 21—Literature Unit

D'Aulaires' Book of Greek Myths

Theseus

1. List the facts in the story that are discussed on the Minoans history card.

_____

_____

_____

_____

Oedipus

1. Explain the answer to the riddle of the Sphinx on p. 158.

_____

_____

2. Oedipus killed his _____ and married his _____. When he realized this he was so upset that he _____.

The Golden Fleece

1. How had Jason earned Hera's help?

_____

_____

2. Why did King Pelias send Jason after the golden fleece?

_____

_____

3. What Bible story is similar to the story about the King of Colchis sacrificing his son?

_____

_____

D'Aulaires' Book of Greek Myths

4. What were the sailors who went with Jason called?

_____

_____

5. Draw a harpy.

6. Who did Eros make to fall in love with Jason?

_____

_____

7. How was Jason able to stand the heat of the fire-breathing bulls?

_____

_____

8. What did Medea do that made all the gods angry at her?

_____

_____

9. Why were the Sirens dangerous?

_____

_____

D'Aulaires' Book of Greek Myths

10. How did King Pelius die?

_____

_____

11. What oath to Medea did Jason break?

_____

_____

12. How did Jason die?

_____

_____

_____

The Calydonian Boar Hunt

1. Who shot the arrow that stopped the Calydonian boar?

_____

_____

2. What was unique about the winner of the Calydonian Boar Hunt?

_____

_____

_____

Apples of Love and the Apple of Discord

1. What happened if you lost a footrace to Atalanta?

_____

_____

_____

HOMER AND GREEK MYTHOLOGY
Project 2, Page 24—Literature Unit

D'Aulaires' Book of Greek Myths

2. What happened if you won a footrace with Atalanta?

_____

_____

3. How did Melanion beat Atalanta?

_____

_____

4. What caused Athena, Hera, and Aphrodite to quarrel?

_____

_____

5. What did Aphrodite promise to Paris if he would choose her?

_____

_____

6. List three facts from the story that are not listed on the Trojan War history card.

_____

_____

_____

_____

HOMER AND GREEK MYTHOLOGY
Project 2, Page 25—Literature Unit

D'Aulaires' Book of Greek Myths
Answers

IN OLDEN TIMES
1. They were created by a folk of shepherds and herdsmen.
2. They looked and acted like humans but were more handsome, could do no wrong, and were immortal
3. Mt. Olympus
4. In their own shape or disguised as humans or animals.
5. Mother Earth
6. Their gods are false and man-made. Our God is true and uncreated

GAEA, MOTHER EARTH
Gaea, the Earth, came out of darkness. Mother Earth married Uranus (the sky) and all living things came from them.

THE TITANS
1. Titans and Titanesses
2. Cyclops (a one-eyed giant)
3. He threw them into a deep pit along with the Cyclops
4. Kill their father
5. see pg. 12
6. Pontus
7. Cronus. He would not set his monstrous brothers free
8. He was afraid one would grow stronger than him
9. see pg. 14
10. Zeus. Rhea gave Cronus a stone to swallow and secretly hid Zeus

ZEUS AND HIS FAMILY
1. nymphs   goat   Amaltheia
2. ambrosia and nectar
3. impenetrable breastplate
4. Metis, goddess of Prudence

5. not to try to overthrow his father on his own
6. Metis, it made him vomit up his children
7. All his children joined Zeus against him
8. Universe   alone   brothers   sisters   Titans   gods   Prometheus   Epimetheus   future   Zeus
9. The sons of Mother Earth. weapons
10. He locked them in Tartarus
11. Titans   Tartarus   terrible monsters   Typhon
12. She hid in a cave and raised Typhon's children

D'Aulaires' Book of Greek Myths

Answers
ZEUS AND HIS FAMILY
Hera
1. jealous
2. he changed her into a cow
3. he had 100 bright eyes on his body
4. he bored Argus to death
5. Hera put them there so people would remember Argus

Hephaestus
1. smiths and fire
2. robots of gold and silver
3. Aphrodite

Aphrodite
1. she had no father or mother
2. Eros
3. she dove into the sea from which she came each year

Ares
1. vain, cruel
2. make trouble between friends
3. he screamed and acted like a child

Athena
1. she sprung fully grown from Zeus' head
2. Mother Earth predicted Metis would have a son that would overthrow Zeus
3. she boasted she learned nothing from Athena
4. spider
5. olive tree
6. she protected it.

Poseidon
1. sea
2. Amphitrite
3. Apollo and Artemis

Apollo
1. chariot pulled by white swans
2. the oracle of Delphi
3. Apollo

Artemis
1. Apollo
2. that he not make her marry
3. he saw Artemis bathing
4. his own hounds killed him
5. they put him in a jar
6. they killed each other with javelins with which they were trying to kill a deer
7. he made him blind
8. Apollo sent a scorpion that stung Orion
9. it was put in the sky as a constellation

Hermes
1. Apollo's
2. he tied branches to their tails to brush out their tracks
3. Apollo's lyre
4. golden hat with wings, winged sandals and cape

Hades
1. he always has room for one more soul
2. Styx
3. Charon
4. the three-headed watchdog of the underworld

Persephone and Demeter
1. never make the earth green again
2. she ate a few pomegranate seeds
3. when Persephone goes to Hades, Fall and Winter comes—when she returns Demeter is happy so Spring and Summer come

HOMER AND GREEK MYTHOLOGY
Project 2, Page 27—Literature Unit

D'Aulaires' Book of Greek Myths

Dionysus
1. she tried to look on Zeus in all his splendor
2. making wine from grape juice
3. dolphins
4. Hestia

MINOR GODS, NYMPHS, SATYRS, AND CENTAURS
Prometheus
1. repopulating the earth with living creatures
2. fire
3. they looked to the heavens and sacrificed to the gods
4. Prometheus covered had covered them with fat
5. an eagle ate out his liver every day

Pandora
1. curiosity   sealed jar   never to open it
2. jar   a horde of miseries
3. hope   put an end to it

Deucalion
1. ark
2. he threw rocks over his shoulders

Eos
1. mother of the four winds
2. eternal life
3. he kept getting older, and he shriveled into a grasshopper

Helios and Phaethon
1. he rode across the sky in his glowing chariot
2. vessel of gold
3. to drive Helios' chariot for one day
4. he threw a thunderbolt at the chariot

Pan
1. he had goat's legs

Echo, Syrinx
and the Wild and Vulgar Centaurs
1. her ability to form her own words
2. her father turned her into a tree
3. a man from the head to the waist then a horses body from the waist down

Asclepius
1. healing the sick
2. Zeus killed him with a thunderbolt

Muses
1. nine
2. all that happened since the beginning of time
3. to sing

Orpheus
1. she was killed by a snake
2. to get his bride
3. Euridice could not leave the underworld

MORTAL DESCENDANTS OF ZEUS
Danaus, Perseus, and the Gorgon
1. 2, 1, 3
   2, 3, 4, 1
2. a. he got the gray sisters to tell where Medusa lived
   b. he looked in the reflection so he wouldn't turn to stone
   c. he put Medusa's head in it
3. they were put in the sky

D'Aulaires' Book of Greek Myths

Clever and Vainglorious Kings
1. he was given ears like a donkey because he voted against Apollo
2. he had to push a rock up a hill so he would be too busy to cause trouble
3. Bellerophon beat Chimera by putting lead in its fiery mouth
4. Melampus was very kind to all animals

Heracles
1. in a fit of rage he killed his children
2. killed 1) monstrous lion 2) hydra 3) boar 4) dangerous birds 5)bring back Artemis' hind 6) clean the stables of Augeas 7) get the girdle of Hippolyta 8) capture man-eating mares 9) catch fire-breathing bull 10) bring herd of red cows

Theseus
1. island of Crete ruled by King Minos
   Palace of Cnossus (Knossos)
   Theseus killed the Minotaur

Oedipus
1. a child crawls on all fours, then stands on two feet, and lastly walks with a cane
2. father   mother   put out his eyes

The Golden Fleece
1. he carried her across the river
2. he thought Jason would be killed trying to get it
3. Abraham and Isaac
4. Argonauts
5. Draw a picture of a fat bird with a woman's head
6. Medea
7. Medea gave him a slave
8. she helped Jason kill her brother
9. if you heard their singing you couldn't leave
10. he got into a boiling caldron thinking he would become young
11. that he would always love her
12. a piece of the Argo fell and hit him in the head

The Calydonian Boar Hunt
1. Atalanta
2. his life would end when the log burned up

Apples of Love and the Apple of Discord
1. you would die
2. you could marry her
3. he threw apples to distract her during the race
4. Eris offered a golden apple to the most beautiful of them
5. he could have the most beautiful woman in the world
6. Aphrodite promised Paris he could have the most beautiful woman in the world; Helen was the daughter of Zeus; Paris and Menelaus fought a duel for Helen, but Aphrodite rescued Paris and the duel was undecided.

HOMER AND GREEK MYTHOLOGY
Project 3

Mythological Gods

On the following two pages you will find the names of each of the twelve major Olympian gods and Hestia. In each space above the name draw a picture of the god or goddess with colored pencils or markers. Under each name write of what they were god or goddess. (Refer to pages 22 and 23 of *D'Aulaires Book of Greek Myths.*)

ZEUS HERA POSEIDON ATHENA

ARES APHRODITE HEPHAESTUS

ARTEMIS

HERMES

DIONYSUS

DEMETER
AND PERSEPHONE

APOLLO

HESTIA

HOMER AND GREEK MYTHOLOGY
Project 4

Zeus' Family Reunion

Plan a special activity to conclude your unit. Have students choose a Greek god or goddess to portray. (It is best to have as many different characters represented as possible.) Using *D'Aulaires Book of Greek Myths* and other references, students will research into their character to write a report. Units 4 and 6 of the *Institutes for Excellence in Writing* (by Andrew Pudewa) give superb guidelines for gathering information and structuring the report. At the Family Reunion students will read their reports.

Consider the following ideas for your family reunion:

Invitation:
Send home invitations to parents in advance. Have students make their own invitations or use the sample one provided.

Costumes:
Have students dress like their character. An example of an easy-to-make-tunic is provided. Also, students may hold a prop that represents their character. (ex. Zeus - lightning bolt or Dionysus - bowl of grapes)

Decorations:
FAMILY TREE: *(see pgs. g06-36)*
Make a large tree. Have the students design an 8" x 11" poster with their god's or goddess's name on it. After reports are read, students will come up to the tree and put their poster on the tree to show their relationship to other characters. Chronus should be placed on the trunk. Zeus and Hera should be posted in the middle of the tree so their children will all fit on the tree. A sketch of a sample tree is included.

DO YOU REMEMBER WHEN:
Make a big mural listing and depicting the students' favorite events from the stories they read.

Food:
Provide ambrosia (see next page) and grape juice as refreshment.

Game:
Make namecards of gods and goddesses. Tape a name to each child's back. The children go to each other and ask questions with only "yes" or "no" answers. The children use the question and answer process to determine the name on their back. When the children guesses the names on their backs they get a new name so the game can continue as long as desired.

HOMER AND GREEK MYTHOLOGY
Project 4, Page 2

Zeus' Family Reunion

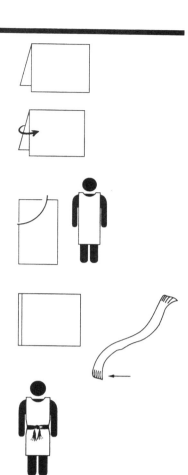

Tunic of the gods
1. Use a piece of 45" fabric. Measure from the shoulder to just below the knee to determine the amount of fabric needed (Approx. 2 yds). Old sheets may be used, too.
2. Fold a two yard length in half as shown on right.
3. Fold 45" width in half as shown on left.
4. Cut out neck hole in the corner with two folds as shown on left. (It's better to cut a second time than to cut too much the first time.)
5. Cut belt from different colored fabric as shown on right. (Approx. 1.5 yards long) Fringe the edge with scissors.
6. Tie belt around waist.
7. Have children wear sandals for shoes.

Ambrosia (Serves 12 to 14)
> 10 valencia or navel oranges
> 1 cup of sugar
> 7 cups of shredded coconut
> Mix together and chill.

YOU ARE CORDIALLY INVITED TO MOUNT OLYMPUS TO A BANQUET FOR THE GODS. FESTIVITIES WILL INCLUDE FOOD AND DRINK AS WELL AS A TIME FOR THE GODS TO REMINISCE ABOUT SOME OF THEIR FAVORITE PAST MEMORIES. MORTALS ARE REMINDED NOT TO GET INVOLVED IN ANY JUDGING OF BEAUTY CONTESTS BETWEEN THE GODDESSES, NOT TO FLIRT WITH ZEUS WHEN HERA IS AROUND, AND NOT TO EAT ANY FRUIT THAT HADES MIGHT OFFER.

NO R.S.V.P. REQUIRED— THE GODS ALREADY KNOW IF YOU ARE COMING.

Family Tree

HOMER AND GREEK MYTHOLOGY
Project 5—Literature Unit

The Children's Homer —Comprehension Questions

Have the children write the answers to these questions on a separate piece of paper. Make sure to use complete sentences.

Part 1

CHAPTER ONE
1. Who is Telemachus?
2. What does it mean when Odysseus was "foreseeing the disasters?"
3. Name, in order, the things that Odysseus did to try to convince the messenger that he was "mad."
4. Why did Odysseus not want to enter the war against Troy?
5. Who is Penelope?

CHAPTER TWO
1. What was the first clue that the stranger was not a threat to Telemachus?
2. What advice did the stranger give to Telemachus concerning his father, Odysseus?
3. Why was the house of Odysseus being wasted away?
4. What is a "wooer?"
5. Name, in order, the different forms that the stranger became.

CHAPTER THREE
1. What caused the change in Telemachus?
2. What does the word "minstrel" mean?
3. Why were the wooers so upset about this council that Telemachus called?
4. Who is Phemius?
5. What did Telemachus think about all night?

CHAPTER FOUR
1. Who is Egyptus, and why did he have tears in his eyes?
2. What is the reason that the herald placed a staff into the hands of Telemachus when he rose to speak?
3. Who is Laertes?
4. What is the purpose of Penelope weaving a wide web of cloth?
5. What is the sign of the two eagles who flew over the place where the council was being held?

CHAPTER FIVE
1. What did the goddess Athene instruct Telemachus to do?
2. Who is the only person Telemachus told of his plans to go to Pylos and Sparta?
3. How did Telemachus manage to get a ship and crew together for his voyage?
4. Alphabetize these words:
darkened   dear   danger   desire   doors
5. What is a "spacious" room?

CHAPTER SIX
1. The greatest of the Cities of men was what city?
2. Describe the city of Troy as sung by the minstrel.
3. Who was the King of Phthia?
4. Who guided the ship of Telemachus and his crew?
5. Who was Helen?

CHAPTER SEVEN
1. What was the first city at which the ship landed?
2. The dark-haired god of the sea was named _____.
3. What words of encouragement did the goddess Athene speak to Telemachus concerning him approaching Nestor?
4. Why did Nestor provide a chariot and horses for Telemachus?
5. What does "reverenced" mean?

HOMER AND GREEK MYTHOLOGY
Project 5, Page 5—Literature Unit

The Children's Homer —Comprehension Questions

CHAPTER EIGHT
1. Name, in order, the five things that Telemachus and Peisistratus did after they were led into the palace.
2. Who came into the high hall just before they had finished their meal?
3. Why did Telemachus begin to weep?
4. Who was Peisistratus' father?
5. Why did Helen give a drug to the men?

CHAPTER NINE
1. Who is Eidothee?
2. When does Proteus come out of the sea?
3. Name three things Proteus became while he was being held.
4. What news of Odysseus did the Ancient One of the Sea bring to Menelaus?
5. What is a "vestibule"?

CHAPTER TEN
1. What does it mean when something or someone is "immortal"?
2. Who is Achilles?
3. The noblest of all men who defended King Priam's city was whom?
4. How did the nymph Thetis hide her son?
5. How did the wise Odysseus find Achilles?

CHAPTER ELEVEN
1. What does it mean when a council was "summoned"?
2. What is a "soothsayer"?
3. What caused the quarrel between Achilles and Agamemnon in the beginning?
4. Who stopped from slaying Agamemnon with his sword?
5. How did this chapter end?

CHAPTER TWELVE
1. What happened to other brave men because of the quarrel between Achilles and Agamemnon?
2. Which goddess had lion's eyes?
3. What does the word "fleeces" mean?
4. Why didn't Agamemnon the king get any sleep?

CHAPTER THIRTEEN
1. A Trojan warrior smote king Agamemnon on the arm. What does that mean?
2. Why didn't king Agamemnon continue to fight in the war?
3. Who was the healer worth the lives of many men?

CHAPTER FOURTEEN
1. Achilles was standing by the stern of his ship. What part is the stern?
2. From where were the Greeks flinging great stones upon the attackers?
3. What was the omen that Hector announced as best?
4. Who is the greatest of the gods?

CHAPTER FIFTEEN
1. Who was the first of the great Trojan Champions to go down before the onset of Patroklos?
2. What does the word "slew" mean?
3. Who was the mother of Achilles?

CHAPTER SIXTEEN
1. Where do the gods dwell?
2. What is the name of the god who was lame and crooked of foot?
3. What is the reason Thetis went to Olympus?

HOMER AND GREEK MYTHOLOGY
Project 5, Page 3—Literature Unit

The Children's Homer —Comprehension Questions

4. Thetis flew down from Olympus like what animal?

CHAPTER SEVENTEEN
1. What does Achilles say to his immortal horses?
2. What is the brightest of all stars, yet is a sign of evil?
3. Summarize this chapter in one complete sentence.

CHAPTER EIGHTEEN
1. What made Helen begin to weep?
2. Who or what did Hector pray to Zeus concerning?
3. What are three triumphs of Hector after he went back into battle?

CHAPTER NINETEEN
1. What was the pledge Hector wanted to make with Achilles?
2. How did Hector die?
3. Where was Hector's mother standing when she witnessed the great fight?

CHAPTER TWENTY
1. Who was the messenger of Zeus?
2. What advice did the messenger give to King Priam?
3. How did Achilles die?
4. Achilles was laid in a grave on what day?

CHAPTER TWENTY ONE
1. Who was the first person to see Hector's father bringing his body back home?
2. Where was the body taken?
3. What took place on the tenth day? On the eleventh day? On the twelfth day?

CHAPTER TWENTY TWO
1. Who won the armor of Achilles?
2. What was the purpose of the great Wooden Horse?
3. How did the Wooden horse get inside the walls of the city?
4. What happened when the warriors came out of the Wooden Horse?

CHAPTER TWENTY THREE
1. What message did Athene give to Telemachus?
2. What gift did Helen give to Telemachus for his mother's keeping?
3. What was the sign of the eagle with a goose in its claws?

Part 2
CHAPTER ONE
1. Who was the god of the sea?
2. Give three characteristics of the Island where Odysseus was being held by the nymph Calypso.
3. What is the reason Calypso gave for keeping Odysseus on the island?
4. What happened to the raft that Odysseus had built?

CHAPTER TWO
1. Who is Nausicaa?
2. What made Odysseus wake up?
3. Alphabetize these words:
people   prayed   pity   princess   palm

CHAPTER THREE
1. The doors of King Alcinous' palace were _____ and the posts were of _____.
2. What did the minstrel sing about?

The Children's Homer —Comprehension Questions

3. Name three games that were played out from the palace.
4. What two games are the Phaenicians perfect in playing?

CHAPTER FOUR
1. Describe what Cyclops looked like.
2. What did the Cyclops eat for his midday meal?
3. What name did Odysseus give to Cyclops as his own?
4. What did the men use as a sacrifice to the gods for helping them escape the Cyclops?

CHAPTER FIVE
1. Who is Eolus?
2. For how long did they sail the West Wind?
3. On which day did Odysseus come in sight of Ithaka?
4. What happened that pushed the ship away from their land?

CHAPTER SIX
1. What lies all around where the Sirens sit?
2. Which is the only ship that ever passed through the island of the Sirens?
3. How did Odysseus keep from getting sucked down into Charybdis?

CHAPTER SEVEN
1. What was King Alcinous' reaction to the story Odysseus told?
2. How did Odysseus finally reach his land?
3. What did the wooers decide to do when they heard that Telemachus had gone to Sparta for help?

CHAPTER EIGHT
1. How did Eumaeus treat Odysseus? Did he know it was really Odysseus?
2. What made Odysseus stay with Eumaeus instead of going into the town to beg?
3. Alphabetize these words: storms should surely swineherd send

THE STORY OF EUMAEUS THE SWINEHERD
1. What does the word "dwelt" mean?
2. What does Laertes do all day long?
3. How did Eumaeus become a swineherd and end up on the island of Ithaka?
4. How did this chapter end?

CHAPTER NINE
1. Who helped Odysseus change his appearance?
2. What did Odysseus appear to be?

CHAPTER TEN
1. What did Telemachus order Eumaeus to do with Odysseus?
2. What are "vagabonds"?
3. What did Antinous do to Odysseus?
4. How did this chapter end?

CHAPTER ELEVEN
1. Why was Irus not happy with Odysseus?
2. What was the prize for the winner of the fight?
3. What did the goddess Athene do to Penelope while she was sleeping?

CHAPTER TWELVE
1. What does the word "neglect" mean?
2. Why did Penelope weep?
3. How did the scar get on the foot of Odysseus?
4. How will Penelope choose which wooer will be her husband?

Homer and Greek Mythology
Project 5, Page 5—Literature Unit

The Children's Homer —Comprehension Questions

CHAPTER THIRTEEN
1. Who was Ctesippus?
2. Why does the second-sighted man leave the house of Odysseus?
3. Alphabetize these words:
mouth   mockery   meat   might   men

CHAPTER FOURTEEN
1. Who is the man that brought the bow to Odysseus?
2. What happened when Odysseus held the bow in his hands?
3. What was scattered at the feet of Odysseus?
4. What was heard outside?

CHAPTER FIFTEEN
1. Who is the first man Odysseus killed with his arrow?
2. Who were the two men helping Odysseus kill the wooers?
3. How did this chapter end?

CHAPTER SIXTEEN
1. How did Penelope finally know that the man truly was Odysseus?

CHAPTER SEVENTEEN - THE FINAL CHAPTER
1. Who did Odysseus decide to visit at the beginning of this chapter?
2. In Laertes' garden were _____ pear trees, _____ apple trees, and _____ fig trees. (Numerical answer)
3. What are "fisherfolk"?
4. How does this story end?

The Children's Homer —Comprehension Questions

Answers
Part I

CHAPTER 1
1. the son of Odysseus
2. he knew that disaster was going to come
3. he yoked two different animals to the same plough, he ploughed the field, then he sowed it, not with seeds, but with salt
4. he had a wife and an infant son that he did not want to leave
5. the wife of Odysseus

CHAPTER 2
1. the stranger left his spear in the spearstand
2. he advised Telemachus to go look for his father
3. because the wooers were waiting for Penelope to decide which man she would marry
4. a person who is wanting to take a woman as his wife
5. woman, then an eagle, then Athene

CHAPTER 3
1. he knew Athene was right and decided in his heart to take the advice
2. a musician who entertains
3. they did not want to leave the house of Odysseus
4. the minstrel
5. he thought of what he would say to the council the next day

CHAPTER 4
1. an older man of the council. Because his son had been killed in the war against Troy, too

2. so that everyone would listen to him
3. the father of Odysseus
4. when she was finished weaving the web, she would have to choose a husband
5. affliction to those who insult the house of Odysseus

CHAPTER 5
1. go back home and wait for a ship and crew to be gathered for his voyage
2. his nurse, Eurycleia
3. Athene gathered them for Telemachus
4. danger darkened dear desire doors
5. lots of room or space

CHAPTER 6
1. Troy
2. high towers, great gates, strong men, well armed, lots of gold and silver
3. Peleus
4. the goddess Athene
5. the fairest woman in the world

CHAPTER 7
1. Pylos
2. Poseidon
3. the right words will come
4. so he could travel on land
5. to have held in high respect

CHAPTER 8
1. they were brought to the bath, they were given cloaks, they dressed themselves, they were led into the King's hall, and they washed their hands
2. Helen
3. he was thinking about his father
4. King Menelaus
5. to stop them from being sad

HOMER AND GREEK MYTHOLOGY
Project 5, Page 7–Literature Unit

The Children's Homer —Comprehension Questions

CHAPTER 9
1. daughter of the Ancient One of the Sea
2. when the sun is highest in the heavens
3. leopard, boar, stream of water, flowering tree
4. that he was alive and being held on an island
5. a part of the house for sleeping quarters

CHAPTER 10
1. it can never age or die
2. the greatest of the heroes who had fought against Troy
3. Hector
4. she dressed him as a maiden
5. he tricked him into picking out a sword instead of a gleaming mirror

CHAPTER 11
1. they were commanded to meet together
2. someone who can tell the future
3. they were fighting over maidens
4. Athene
5. Achilles is still filled with anger for Agamemnon

CHAPTER 12
1. they were killed in the battle
2. Athene
3. a type of cloth; material
4. he could sense the Trojans that were encamped along the plains

CHAPTER 13
1. he hit him with a sword
2. because he was injured
3. Machaon

CHAPTER 14
1. the rear of the ship

2. from the towers that were along the wall
3. "to fight a good fight for our country"
4. Zeus

CHAPTER 15
1. Sarpedon
2. kill
3. Thetis

CHAPTER 16
1. Olympus
2. Hephaistos
3. to beg the gods to make Achilles a new armor
4. hawk

CHAPTER 17
1. bring him home safely from this battle
2. Orion's Dog
3.

CHAPTER 18
1. she was sad over the death of Hector
2. that his infant son would become far greater than his father
3. drover the Greeks back to their ships, affrighted the Greeks with his thousand watchfires, broke through the wall that the Greeks had built

CHAPTER 19
1. if one dies, the other will be able to have his body buried with honor in his own home
2. Achilles slew him in the neck with his sword
3. she was standing on the tower of the wall

HOMER AND GREEK MYTHOLOGY
Project 5, Page 8—Literature Unit

The Children's Homer —Comprehension Questions

CHAPTER 20
1. Iris
2. the messenger told King Priam to go beg for his son's body to be returned to his own home
3. he died by an arrow in battle
4. on the eighth day

CHAPTER 21
1. his sister
2. to his own bed
3. tenth day: they bore brave Hector away, eleventh day: they feasted, twelfth day: the battle began anew

CHAPTER 22
1. Odysseus
2. to finally take the city of Troy
3. the Trojans thought it was amazing so they pushed it inside the walls
4. they slew the whole city and took its treasures

CHAPTER 23
1. to leave and go back home
2. a robe
3. Odysseus would come home and get rid of the wooers
4. Odysseus is on his way home

Part II
CHAPTER 1
1. Poseidon
2. blossoming wood, soft meadows, violets, fountains, clear streams
3. because she loved him
4. the waves shattered it

CHAPTER 2
1. the daughter of the King of the Island
2. Nausicaa was playing loudly with her maidens
3. palm people pity prayed Princess

CHAPTER 3
1. golden, silver
2. Achilles and Odysseus
3. boxing, wrestling, racing, dancing
4. running and dancing

CHAPTER 4
1. giant with one eye in the middle of his forehead
2. two men
3. Noman
4. the sheep of Cyclops

CHAPTER 5
1. lord of the winds
2. nine days
3. on the tenth day
4. the sailors opened the bag with winds blowing here and there

CHAPTER 6
1. bones of men
2. Jason of Argo
3. he grabbed onto a branch

CHAPTER 7
1. he offered Odysseus a ship straight home
2. King Alcinous' ship brought him home
3. they took a ship to find and kill him

CHAPTER 8
1. he treated him kind; no
2. Eumaeus told him of the wooers

The Children's Homer —Comprehension Questions

3. send should storms surely swineherd

THE STORY OF EUMAEUS THE SWINEHERD
1. to live among
2. he sits and thinks about Odysseus
3. he was sold by a traitor
4. Telemachus came home

CHAPTER 9
1. Athene
2. an old beggar

CHAPTER 10
1. take him into town to beg
2. homeless travelers
3. he hit him with a chair
4. Odysseus was sitting on the threshold of his own house

CHAPTER 11
1. because he was another beggar
2. becoming the only beggar allowed in Ithaka, and some pudding
3. made her look like her youth and beautiful

CHAPTER 12
1. to abandon, to leave
2. she missed her husband
3. attack of a boar
4. whoever could bend the great bow of Odysseus

CHAPTER 13
1. the rudest and roughest wooer of them all
2. because he could sense trouble
3. meat men might mockery mouth

CHAPTER 14
1. Eumaeus
2. he bent the great bow
3. bronze-weighted arrows
4. thunder

CHAPTER 15
1. Antinous
2. Telemachus and Eumaeus
3. the women found out that Odysseus was alive

CHAPTER 16
1. he described the bed that he had made

CHAPTER 17
1. his father, Laertes
2. 13; 10; 40
3. men who fish; fishermen
4. Odysseus is home with his family happily ever after

HOMER AND GREEK MYTHOLOGY
Project 6

The instructions for this project can be found on Appendix 2-1.

Homer and Mycenean Civilization

I

The Mycenean Greeks built a very impressive, and powerful civilization. In fact, the king of one neighboring civilization that was much larger, the Hittites, was even a little afraid of them. Much of what we know about them is a result of archaeology, a science that involves digging up ancient ruins to see what we can learn about ancient people. Some of the most amazing ruins that archaeologists have dug up to learn about ancient Mycenean civilization are the ruins of Mycenae and Tyrns, which were important Mycenean fortresses, and Troy, where they fought an important war. Mycenae and Tyrns are so impressive that later Greeks thought that they couldn't have been built by normal people. They told a story that they were built with the help of the Cyclops, a very big giant with one eye.

II

But how, you may ask, did the archaeologists know where to dig? The answer is that many of them used their knowledge of ancient Greek myths, legends and stories. The most important source of those stories is Homer. In fact, the most famous archaeologist to explore Greek civilization, Heinrich Schlieman, who was from Germany, was an avid fan of Homer. Back in the 1800s, many experts thought that Homer had probably just made up all of those wonderful stories, but Schlieman was determined to prove them wrong. He was the first archaeologist to discover the ruins of Mycenae and Troy, and he did mainly by using his detailed, scholarly knowledge of Homer.

III

The works that inspired Schlieman were Homer's epic poems The Iliad, and The Odyssey. An epic poem is a very long poem that tells exciting stories about warriors and great men. The Iliad is a story that takes place during the Trojan War, though it doesn't actually include the famous story of the Trojan Horse. It is actually about a bitter argument that develops between Agamemnon, the high king of the Greeks, and Achilles, their greatest leader and warrior, and it ends right before the end of the war. The Odyssey is about another great leader, Oddyseus, about his difficult journey home and about his difficult homecoming. Homer's epics were considered the single most important piece of literature in ancient Greece and many young boys had them nearly memorized by the time their education was finished. Of course, as the story of Schlieman shows us, many modern people had similar feelings for them.

HOMER AND GREEK MYTHOLOGY
Project 6, Page 2

Vocabulary

1. *civilization:*

2. *archaeology:*

3. *ruin:*

4. *myth:*

5. *legend:*

6. *detailed:*

7. *scholarly:*

8. *epic:*

9. *ancient:*

10. *literature:*

HOMER AND GREEK MYTHOLOGY
Project 6, Page 3

Key Word Outline:

I. _____

    1. _____

    2. _____

    3. _____

    4. _____

    5. _____

    6. _____

II. _____

    1. _____

    2. _____

    3. _____

    4. _____

    5. _____

    6. _____

    7. _____

III. _____

    1. _____

    2. _____

    3. _____

    4. _____

    5. _____

    6. _____

    7. _____

HOMER AND GREEK MYTHOLOGY
Project 6, Page 4

Answers
Vocabulary
1. *civilization:* the way in which a people or a nation thinks, lives and organizes itself
2. *archaeology:* the science that studies the remains of past people
3. *ruin:* something that has fallen apart or been buried with age
4. *myth:* a traditional story, usually one that explains certain things that civilization thinks are very important
5. *legend:* a very old story that may be believed to be true, but is usually only partly true
6. *detailed:* very thorough
7. *scholarly:* showing much study and learning
8. *epic:* a long poem about heroic characters
9. *ancient:* very old
10. *literature:* writing that is seen to have artistic or educational value

Key Word Outline:
I. Title: The Myceneasns
   1. Myceneans built civilization
   2. Hitites afraid
   3. Know archaeology ruins
   4. Amazing Mycenae Tyrns
   5. Impressive couldn't normal
   6. Built Cyclops giant

II. Title: Homer and Schlieman
   1. How archaeologists know
   2. Used knowledge stories
   3. Most important Homer
   4. Famous Schlieman fan
   5. Experts though made up
   6. Schlieman determined prove
   7. First to discover Troy

III. Title: Homer's epic poems
   1. Inspired Schlieman poems
   2. Epic exciting warriors
   3. Illiad Trojan War
   4. Argument Agamemnon Achilles
   5. Oddysey difficult journey
   6. Epics important literature
   7. Modern similar feelings

HOMER AND GREEK MYTHOLOGY
Test

1. At what time is it believed that Homer lived?

   _____

   _____

2. What did Homer do for a living? What was this profession called?

   _____

   _____

3. Name two stories Homer composed.

   _____

   _____

4. What physical problem did Homer have?

   _____

   _____

5. Did the Greeks believe in the God of the Bible?

   _____

   _____

6. Name three Greek gods? For what were they known?

   _____

   _____

7. How did the Greeks think their gods were similar to humans?
   How did they think they were different?

   _____

   _____

8. Did the Greeks ever see or hear from any of their gods?

   _____

   _____

HOMER AND GREEK MYTHOLOGY
Test, Page 2

Review

1. What was the first European civilization? From what did they receive their name?

   _____

   _____

2. Describe a Mycenaen citadel. What was it's purpose?

   _____

   _____

   _____

3. What story is about the Trojan War? Who wrote it?

   _____

   _____

   _____

4. Why did God divide Israel into two kingdoms?

   _____

   _____

   _____

5. Name the events studied to date in chronological order including dates and Scripture
   references (where applicable).

   _____

   _____

   _____

   _____

   _____

   _____

THE OLYMPICS
Worksheet

1. What is the approximate date of the first Olympics?

   _____

   _____

2. What was the purpose of the Olympics?

   _____

   _____

3. The Olympic festival was so _____ that warring tribes would stop
   _____ during the games.

4. Who was allowed to participate in the Olympics?

   _____

   _____

5. Fill in what occurred on each day of the Olympics.

   Day one: _____

   _____

   Days two to four: _____

   _____

   _____

   Day five: _____

   _____

6. What did the winner of an event receive at the ceremony? At home afterwards?

   _____

   _____

   _____

THE OLYMPICS
Project

The Olympian Games

There was one thing in which the Greeks were united, and that was the games, in which no one who was not a Greek could take part. The most famous were held at Olympia in Elis. Through all the changes in the different states these had been continued, and they were regarded as being so sacred that no matter how fiercely two Greek tribes might be fighting, they always had a truce during the time of the Olympian games and the days allowed for going and returning. No Greek who could afford to make the journey would think of losing a celebration of the games; and the roads leading to Olympia must have been a wonderfully interesting sight for a week or two before and after the midsummer days on which the festival was held.

Ruins of Entrance to the
Foot-Race Course at Olympia

Imagine the first day of the celebration! The different states had all sent representatives. and these men wore their richest garments and rode in the handsomest chariots that could be obtained. The Greeks enjoyed processions so much that there can hardly fail to have been a parade of these, and after it there was almost certainly a solemn sacrifice to Zeus. Then came the important work of making sure that those who wished to engage in the games had a right to do so. Not only the athletes, but the umpires and trainers, had to swear that they were free-born Greeks of unmixed blood, and that they would obey the rules of the games. Even with this oath, they had also to prove their citizenship and the athletes had to show that they had followed the rules of diet and training required. All this would occupy one day from morning till night. The following days - three and perhaps more were given to the contests. There were racing, wrestling, boxing, leaping, throwing of quoits, and hurling of javelins. Last of all were the famous races of four-horse chariots. When the moment had come, there was a loud blast on the trumpets, the barriers fell, and the horses darted forward, while the crowd shouted and cheered in the wildest excitement.

The fifth day was given up to the victors. A boy was sent to the sacred grove to cut with a golden knife branches from a wild olive tree. These were made into wreaths, which were presented to the successful men. It was the proudest moment of a man's life when the herald called his name, his father's name, and that of his native city, and he stepped forward to receive his crown. The crowds shouted their applause, and he forgot the long, weary months of training and thought only of the fame that he had won.

The olive wreath with all that it stood for was reward enough, but there were many more honors awaiting its happy wearer. He usually made a sacrifice to Zeus, and in this all his countrymen who were present were glad to join, for he had brought glory to their country. While the sacrifice was burning, they marched around the altar in a splendid procession, singing choruses of praise to the gods to the music of the flute and the cithara. This was only the beginning, for the sacrifice was followed by numerous banquets. The city that presided at the games gave feasts to the victors, and the victors gave feasts to their friends. Even this was not all, for often a statue in honor of the successful man was set up at Olympia, and maybe another at his own home. Even the return of a victor to his native city was a splendid sight. He was dressed in a rich purple robe, and brought to his home in a chariot drawn by four white horses. His friends and relatives followed him, all in their holiday garments; and then came a crowd, singing and cheering and shouting at the top of their voices. When they had come to the walls, the procession stopped. "What need of walls of defense for a city that has such men as he?" the people cried; and then a piece of the city wall was torn down and the four white horses pranced over the

The Wrestlers

ruins. Of course banquets followed, and often a generous gift of gold and silver. The philosophers of the day sometimes reminded the citizens that these victors in the games were of small value to the state. "They are of no use in peace," declared the wise men, "for not their minds but their bodies have been trained; and they are of no use in war, for their training is so one-sided that they soon break down if they attempt military service." Nevertheless, the worship of the athlete continued. In some places he dined every day at the expense of the city, and all the rest of his life had a front seat reserved for him in the theatre. His name was carefully inscribed on the register that was kept at Olympia, and he was honored as long as he lived. The Greeks had so much regard for these games that they dated events from them, counting the year of a celebration and the following three years as an "Olympiad." For instance, 776 B.C. they called the first year of the first Olympiad; 770 B.C., the third year of the second Olympiad. For more than a thousand years these games were continued without a break. Their influence upon Greek life can hardly be rated too highly. They affected commerce, for where so many thousand people were gathered together, there must have been a vast amount of buying and selling. They affected art, for at the games the sculptor could find the finest of living models. They affected the manners of the people, their regard for religious rites, and also their interest in literature and oratory; for at most of the games contests in these lines also were held. The Greeks never

The Olympia Foot-Race

became-united into one nation, but the games did much to make them feel that they had interests in common, and that if a tribe called in the aid of a foreigner against another tribe, it was in some degree a traitor to the country.

THE OLYMPICS
Project, Page 3

Check out books from your local library on the modern Olympics. Compare the modern Olympics to the original games by either writing or discussing the similarities and differences.

_____

_____

_____

_____

_____

_____

_____

_____

_____

_____

_____

_____

_____

_____

_____

_____

_____

_____

_____

_____

_____

_____

_____

THE OLYMPICS
Project 2

Olympic Field Day

Costume Materials
Inexpensive muslin cut into 42" squares plus a belt of 4" x 60" of the same material (Two squares and one belt for each child).
Large safety pins
Beads (with the hole large enough to fit over the saftey pin)
Markers
Green pipe cleaners
Two copies of "leaf sheet" per person (see below)
Green construction paper

Costume Instructions

  Give each child two squares of muslin and one belt.

 Have the student draw and color a border with markers on the belt and the bottom of each square piece.

 Fill pointed side of eight safety pins with beads.

 Close each one over an empty safety pin. Use empty pin to attach the two muslin squares at shoulders.

 Tie belt at waist.

THE OLYMPICS
Project 2, Page 2

Costume Instructions (Contd.)

Photocopy enough leaves onto green construction paper to make a wreath (20 per wreath). Cut them out. Take pipe cleaners, connect them by twisting and make a circle that rests comfortably on the student's head. Cut additional green pipe cleaner to three inch length (10 per student). Glue leaves to each end of 3" pipe cleaner and allow to dry. Twist onto "head band" into the shape illustrated. Make enough wreaths to give one per victor of the events on the following page.

THE OLYMPICS
Project 2, Page 3

Events
The following events are suggested for your Olympic games:

50 yard dash

1/4 mile race

Long jump

Softball throw

Frisbie throw

Civilized wrestling.
   Have the two competing students place the outside of their right feet together and join right hands. At the whistle they may pull and push the other until one moves his right foot. The remaining competitor is the victor. Competitors may not touch each other with their left hands but may move their left foot to keep their balance.
You may want to separate boys and girls for the competition.

Awards
Have a "herald" award all winners with a wreath by calling out his father's name and the name of the city he is from while someone else places the wreath on his head. The winner should then give thanks to God, not Zeus, as he recognizes that God has blessed him with these gifts.

THE OLYMPICS
Test

1. When did the first Olympics occur?

   _____

   _____

2. Why were the Olympics held?

   _____

   _____

3. Who was permitted to participate in the Olympic games?

   _____

   _____

4. How long did the Olympics last each time they were held?

   _____

   _____

5. Describe what happened each day.

   _____

   _____

   _____

   _____

   _____

6. What did winners receive at the end? What did they do during the victory ceremony?

   _____

   _____

   _____

THE OLYMPICS
Test, Page 2

Review

1. Where was the largest Minoan palace built?

_____

_____

2. From where did the Mycenaen culture receive its name?

_____

_____

3. Describe the legend of the Trojan War.

_____

_____

_____

_____

_____

4. From what did the Phoenicians receive their name?

_____

_____

_____

5. Including dates, list in chronological order all events studied to date.

_____

_____

_____

_____

_____

_____

FOUNDING OF ROME
Worksheet

1. What is the approximate date of the founding of Rome?

   _____

   _____

2. What is the legend about the founding of Rome?

   _____

   _____

   _____

   _____

   _____

3. Who actually founded Rome?

   _____

   _____

4. Who was the largest group of people living in Italy when Rome was begun?
   What was their spoken language?

   _____

   _____

   _____

   _____

5. Who were the first citizens of Rome?

   _____

   _____

   _____

FOUNDING OF ROME
Project

Legend of Rome Comic Strip

The Legends of the Seven Kings of Rome

In Troy, a famous town of Asia Minor, there once lived a man named Aeneas. For ten long years the Greeks, fierce enemies of the Trojans, had been trying to take the city; and at length they succeeded. They set fire to it, and soon the whole town was in flames. Aeneas fought as long as there was any hope in fighting, then he took his aged father on his shoulders, and keeping fast hold of the hand of his little son Ascanius, he fled through the burning streets and over the ruins of the walls to the country. Many of his friends joined him, and they hid away together among the mountains. After a while the gods told Aeneas to build some boats and set out on the sea, for he and his companions must make a new home for themselves in Italy.

They obeyed and set sail, and after many troubles and adventures they reached the Italian shores. Aeneas married Lavinia, the daughter of the king of Latium, and afterward became ruler of that province. He built a town which he named La-vin'i-um, in honor of his wife. After he died Ascanius ruled; but he soon found that his town was becoming too crowded. He concluded, therefore, to leave it and build another on a ridge of a neighboring hill. This he named Alba Longa, or the long white city.

For three hundred years the descendants of Ascanius ruled in Latium. Then there was trouble. The rightful king was Numitor, but his brother Amulius stole the kingdom and murdered Numitor's son. There was also a daughter, Rhea Sylvia, but Amulius disposed of her by making her a priestess of the goddess Vesta. One day Amulius was told that his niece had twin sons whose father was the war god Mars. "If they are allowed to live, they will grow, up and claim the kingdom," thought Amulius; so he put Rhea Sylvia to death and ordered one of his men to throw the boys into the river Tiber. The man obeyed, but the river had overflowed its banks, and when it went down again, it left the two babies on dry land at the foot of the Palatine Hill, not drowned by any means, but exceedingly hungry and crying with all their might. A she wolf coming for a drink heard the crying and went to the children. She seemed to think they were some new kind of cub, for she carried them to her den and nursed them there for some time. At length they were discovered by a shepherd named Faustulus. He frightened the wolf away and carried the babies home to his wife. When Romulus and Remus, as they were called, had grown up, Faustulus told them that they were not his children, but the grandsons of Numitor, and that Numitor was the rightful king. Then the young men and their shepherd friends overcame the wicked Amulius. He was put to death, and the kingdom was given back to Numitor.

The two brothers determined to form a kingdom for themselves, and to build a city near the place where they had been thrown into the water. But now there was trouble, for it was fitting that the elder brother should give his name to the city, and they were twins! Let the gods decide," they said. So Romulus climbed the Palatine Hill and Remus the Aventine, and they watched all day and all night; but the gods gave them no sign. Just at sunrise, however, Remus saw six vultures fly across the sky. His followers shouted with delight and hailed him as king. While they were still shouting, the friends of Romulus cried out joyfully; for, behold, Romulus had seen a flight of twelve vultures! But who could say whether it was worth more to see six birds first or twelve birds second?

The question seems to have been settled in some way in favor of Romulus, for he began to build on the Palatine Hill a wall for a town. Remus jumped over it and said scornfully, "That is what your enemies will do." "And this is the way they will fare," retorted Romulus, and struck his brother angrily. Remus fell down dead, and all his life Romulus grieved for the brother whom he had slain in a moment of anger.

The walls were completed and the place was named Rome; but it needed people. "I will admit as citizens whoever choose to come," said Romulus; and at this, there came crowds of men who had fled from their enemies or from justice. Romulus took them in and protected them.

Rome became strong, but the men of the neighboring states looked upon it scornfully and would not allow their daughters to marry Romans. "If you want wives to match your men," they said to Romulus, "you would better open an asylum for women slaves and thieves and outcasts."

Romulus kept his temper, and a little later he even invited his scornful neighbors to some games in honor of Neptune. All were curious to see the new city, and they did not wait for any urging. The Sabines especially came in full numbers and brought their wives and children also. The Romans entertained them hospitably, and soon the guests were all eagerly watching the games. Suddenly the Romans rushed upon their visitors, seized the young maidens among them, and carried them away to become their wives.

Then the Romans fought with one tribe after another, –with the Sabines last of all, because these people waited till they were fully prepared to fight. The most important thing for the Sabines to do was to take the Roman citadel, that is, the strong fortress which Romulus had built on a hill to protect the city, and they secretly asked the young girl Tarpeia, daughter of the Roman commander, what reward she would demand to let them in. "Give me what you wear on your left arms," she replied, pointing to their heavy golden bracelets. They agreed and she opened the gate. But they also carried their shields upon their left arms, and they felt such scorn for the disloyal maiden that they threw these upon her, and so crushed her to death. That is why the cliff on one side of the ledge on which the citadel stood is called the Tarpeian Rock. For many years afterward, traitors were punished by being hurled from this very cliff.

When the Sabines were once within the city, a savage fight followed between them and the Romans; but now the stolen women had a word to say. Their husbands had treated them kindly and they had become fond of their new homes. They ran fearlessly into the battle, straight between the angry fighters, and begged on the one side their fathers, and on the other their husbands, not to murder one another. The men were so amazed that they stopped fighting, and after a parley they agreed to make peace and even to dwell together as one nation.

After reading the above, use the following pages to create a comic strip about the legend of Romulus and Remus.

FOUNDING OF ROME
Test

1. What is the approximate date of the founding of Rome?

   _____

   _____

2. Who are Romulus and Remus? Tell their story.

   _____

   _____

   _____

   _____

3. Who were the Etruscans?

   _____

   _____

4. What was the spoken language of the largest group of people living in Italy?
   Who were these people?

   _____

   _____

   _____

5. Who were the first citizens of Rome?

   _____

   _____

Review

1. How did Minoans travel? For what reason did they travel?

   _____

   _____

   _____

FOUNDING OF ROME
Test, Page 2

2. What is the date the Trojan Wars supposedly occurred?

_____

_____

3. What was the most important contribution to civilization by the Phoenicians (Canaanites)?

_____

_____

4. Who was the King of Israel when it was divided into two kingdoms?

_____

_____

5. Including dates, list in chronological order all events studied to date.

_____

_____

_____

_____

_____

_____

_____

_____

_____

_____

_____

_____

_____

GREECE COLONIZED, DEMOCRACY BEGINS
Worksheet

1. What is the approximate date of the colonization of Greece?

   _____

   _____

2. How did the colonization of Greece begin?

   _____

   _____

3. Where did the colonies develop?

   _____

   _____

   _____

4. Ancient Greece was composed of _____ _____.

5. Who often fought for control of the states?

   _____

   _____

6. What was *demokratia*? Describe it. Who introduced it to Athens?

   _____

   _____

   _____

   _____

7. Who voted on all matters of government?

   _____

   _____

   _____

8. Who were the *strategoi?*

_____

_____

9. What form of government are the Greeks credited with beginning?

_____

_____

_____

_____

GREECE COLONIZED, DEMOCRACY BEGINS
Project

Booklet of Greek Democracy

Using the cover page below and the following pages to create a booklet that describes and illustrates the main features of early Greek democracy in Athens. Helpful resources include *Illustrated World History, The Greeks* (pages 60, 61) and *Eyewitness Books, Ancient Greece* (page 18). The student should use pictures and text to describe each of the governmental groups.

Have the students read their completed booklet to the class. The teacher may want to ask questions of the students to assure more thorough understanding.

DEMOCRACY IN GREECE

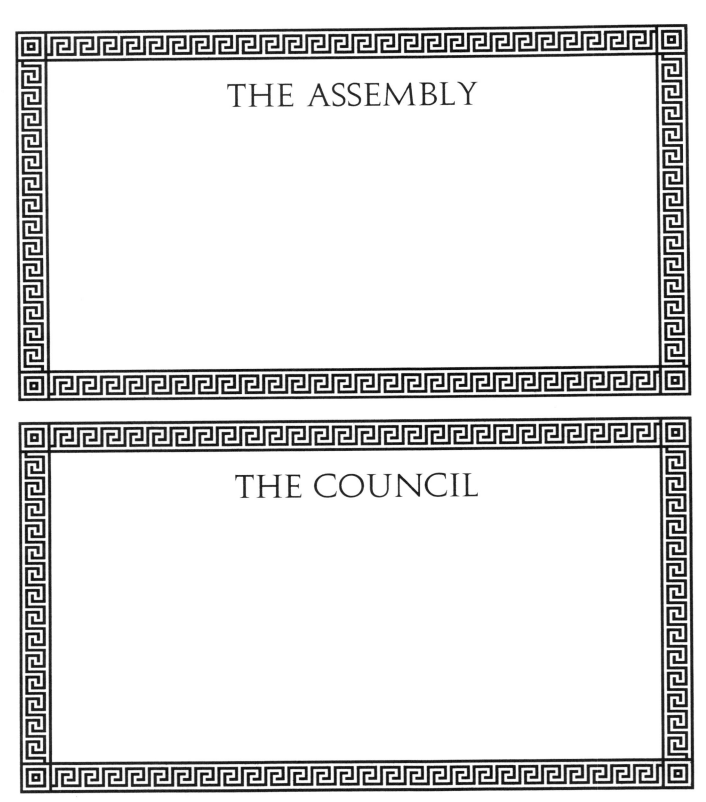

THE ASSEMBLY

THE COUNCIL

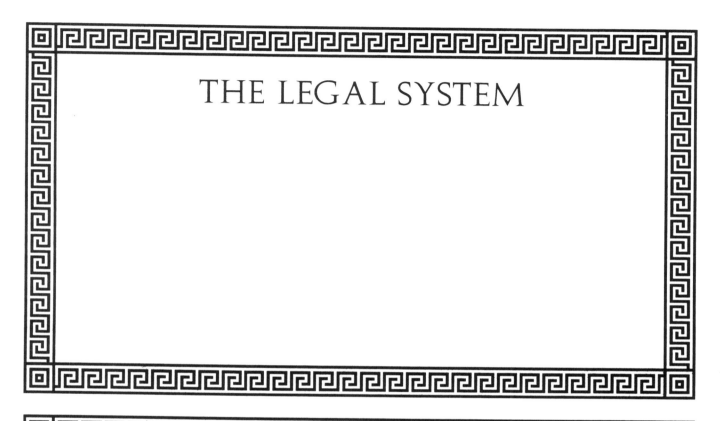

THE LEGAL SYSTEM

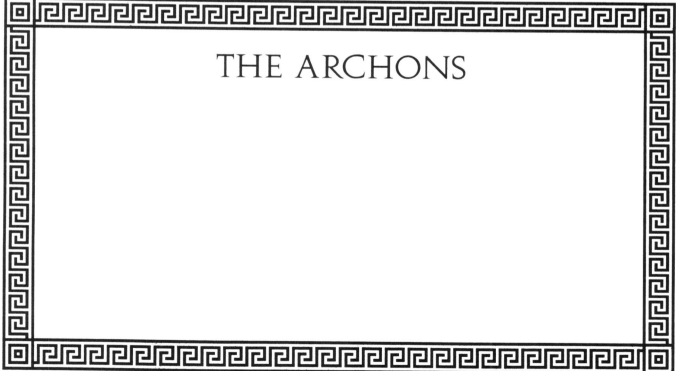

THE ARCHONS

THE STRATEGOI

GREECE COLONIZED, DEMOCRACY BEGINS
Project 2

School Government Excercise

Select two or three students to act as the *Council.* Ask them to come up with a proposal for the rest of the class who will vote on the proposal as the *Assembly.* Encourage discussion at both levels. Several ideas for the Council to consider are:

a. New rules for a favorite playground game

b. How to handle a certain bad behavior

c. How to determine the order for standing in line for something

You may find it good and necessary to explain that the classroom is a benevolent monarchy and not a democracy should some of the ideas not be consistent with your rules and expectations.

GREECE COLONIZED, DEMOCRACY BEGINS

Project 3

Ionic Capital

Doric, Ionic and Corinthian columns developed in Greek architecture. The best examples of Ionic columns can now be found at the Acropolis. This style is lighter and more delicate than the Doric style column, bearing a resemblance to a stylized palm tree.

Supplies

18 oz. oatmeal canister
2 toilet paper tubes
8 popsicle sticks
7.5" x 4.5" sheet of thin cardboard
2" x 8" sheet of thin cardboard
masking tape
glue
acrylic paint and sand
    or, Fleckstone™ paint

Directions

Glue the toilet paper tubes and cardboard strip to oatmeal canister as shown.
Glue 7.5" x 4.5" cardboard sheet across top.
Tape over the ends of the tubes.
Paste on popsicle sticks around canister, spacing evenly.
Paint column with a combination of grays, black and white acrylic paint with a pinch of sand in the paint for texture. Sponges are good to use for a modeled effect. Or, use Fleckstone™ paint for a stone-like finish. Add details in black acrylic paint and let dry.

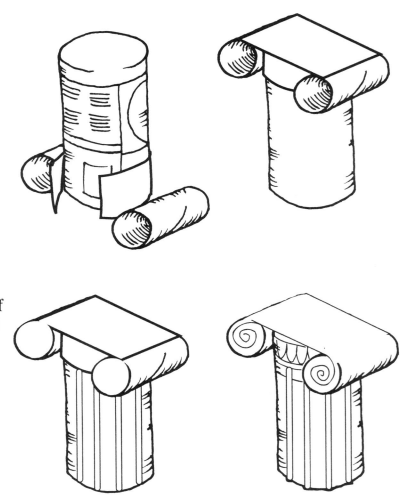

GREECE COLONIZED, DEMOCRACY BEGINS
Test

1. What is the approximate date of the colonization of Greece?

   _____

   _____

2. Describe how the colonization of Greece began. Where did the colonies develop?

   _____

   _____

   _____

3. Who fought for control of the Greek city states?

   _____

   _____

4. What form of government did Cleisthenes introduce to Athens in 508 B.C.? Describe it.

   _____

   _____

   _____

   _____

5. What were the military leaders called?

   _____

   _____

6. Where does today's democracy find its roots?

   _____

   _____

   _____

Review

1. What are the approximate dates of the Minoan culture?

   _____

   _____

2. What was found at Athens and Thebes that has aided our understanding of

   the Myceneans?

   _____

   _____

3. What is the translation of the Greek word "phoinos?"

   _____

   _____

4. Why was Israel divided?

   _____

   _____

5. Name the events studied to date in chronlogical order.

ISRAEL AND JUDAH FALL
Worksheet

1. What do we mean when we say a nation "fell?"

   _____

   _____

2. When did Israel fall? When did Judah fall?

   _____

   _____

   _____

3. Why did these nations fall? How do we know this is the reason?

   _____

   _____

   _____

   _____

4. Where in Scripture do we find these events recorded?

   _____

   _____

5. To what nation did Israel fall? To what nation did Judah fall?

   _____

   _____

   _____

   _____

ISRAEL AND JUDAH FALL
Project

Read II Kings 17 & 25. Using complete sentences, write a paragraph describing why God caused the fall of His nation.

_____

_____

_____

_____

_____

_____

_____

_____

_____

_____

_____

ISRAEL AND JUDAH FALL
Project 2

Read the paragraph below with your students and discuss it with them as they color the woodcut from the 1479 Cologne Bible..

Ahaz at the Altar; Hoshea in Captivity

Ahaz was a weak king of Judah who made sacrifices to foreign gods. He changed the sacred arrangements of the great temple and installed a new type of altar he had seen among the Assyrians. Ahaz was just one of many kings in Judah and in Israel who could no longer protect their people against their powerful neighbors. About a hundred years after the death of Elisha, the kingdom of Israel, under its last king, Hoshea, was conquered by the Assyrians and the people led off into captivity in Assyria. About a hundred and thirty years after that, Judah was defeated by the Babylonians, Solomon's temple was destroyed, and the people carried off to Babylon. 17 (2 Kings 16, & 25)

ISRAEL AND JUDAH FALL
Test

1. What do we mean when we say a nation "fell?"

   _____

   _____

2. What is the date when Israel fell? What is the date when Judah fell?

   _____

   _____

3. Why did these nations fall? How do we know this is the reason?

   _____

   _____

4. What is the Scripture reference for the fall of Israel and Judah?

   _____

   _____

5. To what nation did Israel fall? To what nation did Judah fall?

   _____

   _____

Review

1. What title did the Greeks use for king during the Minoan period that was the similar to a Pharaoh in Egypt?

   _____

   _____

2. Who wrote the poem about the Trojan War? What was it called?

   _____

   _____

3. Approximately when was Israel divided?

   _____

   _____

4. Who was permitted to participate in the ancient Olympics?

   _____

   _____

5. List the events studied to date in chronological order. Include dates and
   Scripture references where applicable.

   _____

   _____

   _____

   _____

   _____

   _____

   _____

   _____

   _____

   _____

PROPHETS OF GOD
Worksheet

1. What are the approximate dates that prophets were regularly used by God?

   _____

   _____

2. Why did God continue to send prophets to His people?

   _____

   _____

3. Next to each prophet fill in each category.

Prophet	*Date*	*King/Kingdom*
Joel		
Hosea		
Amos		
Micah		
Isaiah		
Nahum		
Zephaniah		
Habakkuk		

PROPHETS OF GOD
Project

Using complete sentences, write a paragraph describing one of the visions of Isaiah. Be sure to include the Scripture reference.

_____
_____
_____
_____
_____
_____
_____
_____
_____
_____

PROPHETS OF GOD
Project 2

Prophet Concentration

Directions:
1. Copy and cut out the cards
2. Divide into teams, preferably ones that are as evenly matched as possible
3. Shuffle cards. Lay cards with events showing down and match Prophet sets.
4. Keep score

Notes:
1. The first sheet of cards contains all nine prophets listed on the back of the card, along with their dates and the kingdoms to which their messages were directed.
2. The second sheet contains other information about six of the prophets (two are repeated). Look in Scripture for the answers to whom the prophets prophecied.
3. The final sheet is a blank one which can be used for the children to add new cards, time permitting.

JOEL	HOSEA	AMOS
MICAH	ISAIAH	HABAKKUK
ZEPHANIAH	NAHUM	JONAH

ISRAEL *c.760*	**ISRAEL** *c. 760 - 720*	**JUDAH** *c.835*
JUDAH *c.609*	**JUDAH** *c.739 - 635*	**BOTH** *c.737 - 690*
ASSYRIA (NINEVAH) *c.850*	**ASSYRIA (NINEVAH)** *c.650*	**JUDAH** *c.640*

JOEL	HOSEA	AMOS
MICAH	JOEL	HOSEA
ZEPHANIAH	NAHUM	MICAH

Prophesied to all Israel against injustice and pagan religious practice	*Prophesied from the reign of Jeroboam II to that of Hoshea*	*Prophesied during the reign of Joash the boy-king*
Prophesied against Israel's unfaithfulness	*Called the "Son of Bethuel"*	*Was a contemporary of Isaiah*
Attacked the leaders and the upper class for injustice	*Prophesied against Assyria, Judah's greatest enemy*	*Called on Judah to abandon paganism and seek the Lord*

PROPHETS OF GOD
Project 2, Page 6

PROPHETS OF GOD
Test

1. What are the approximate dates of the prophets of God?

    _____

    _____

2. What was God's purpose in sending His prophets to His people?

    _____

    _____

    _____

    _____

3. List three prophets discussed on the card. Tell under whom they were king and to
    whom they prophesied.

    _____

    _____

    _____

    _____

    _____

    _____

    _____

PROPHETS OF GOD
Test, Page 2

Review

1. Describe the legend of the Trojan War?

_____

_____

_____

_____

2. What was the relationship between the Canaanites and the Phoenicians?

_____

_____

_____

3. Who was permitted to participate in the Olympic games?

_____

_____

4. Who was king when Israel was divided? Who became ruler of each kingdom?

_____

_____

_____

5. List in chronological order all the events studied to date.

   Next to each list the appropriate dates and Scripture references where applicable.

_____

_____

_____

_____

_____

_____

ROMAN REPUBLIC DEVELOPED
Worksheet

1. What are the approximate dates of the "Roman Republic Developed?"

    _____

    _____

2. After the Romans broke away from the Etruscan king what form of government did they establish?

    _____

    _____

    _____

3. What were the leaders of this new government called? How did they receive their position?

    _____

    _____

    _____

4. What were the two classes of Romans?   Describe each one.

    _____

    _____

5. What did strife between the two classes cause?

    _____

    _____

6. What relationship does the United States form of government have with the Roman republic?

    _____

    _____

ROMAN REPUBLIC DEVELOPED
Project

Roman Government Outline

On the following pages you will find
worksheets to aid in the understanding of
the government structure in the Roman
republic.

Using the *The Usborne Illustrated World
History, the Romans,* pages 10 and 11 fill in
the blanks of the text and fill in the job
descriptions of each of the various
officials.

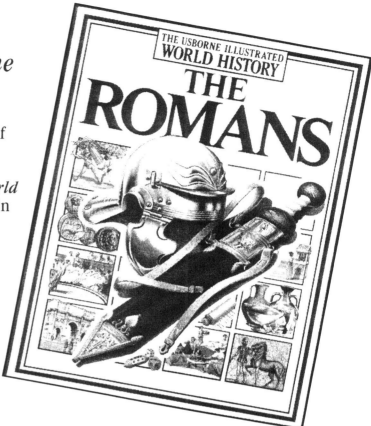

ROMAN REPUBLIC DEVELOPED
Project, Page 2

The Government of the Roman Republic

Rome was governed by the _____, originally a group of 100 _____ who were from _____ families. The patricians were the _____ citizens. The senators voted in an election known as an _____, to elect senators to be _____ officials. Below, please see the various elected and appointed officials.

2 _____

Job Description:

8 _____

Job Description:

2 _____

Job Description:

ROMAN REPUBLIC DEVELOPED
Project, Page 3

4 _____

Job Description:

20 _____

Job Description:

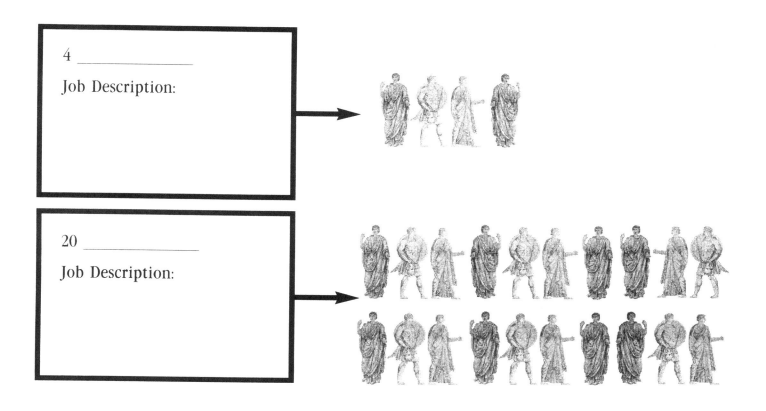

Dictator (temporary)

Job Description:

Magister Equitum

Job Description:

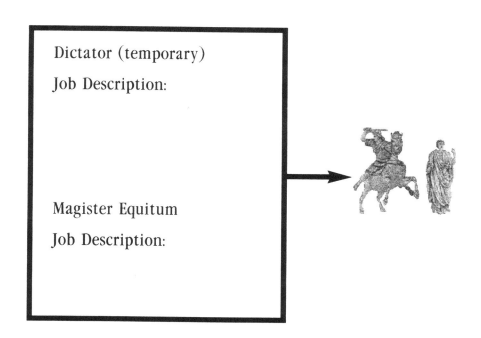

ROMAN REPUBLIC DEVELOPED
Project 2

Assign the various offices to each of the students in your class and ask them to write a fictitious account of a specific time period of the life in "public office." You may even want to describe a particular political environment for them to have just "lived through" to stimulate their imaginations. You may use the following page for this assignment.

CIRCUMSTANCES TO CONSIDER FOR THIS MIGHT INCLUDE:

a time of peace

a time of war

anticipating an upcoming election and running for office

preparing for certain holidays

You might have different circumstances for different roles to broaden the classes' collective understanding. After completing the write up of their "diary" consider having them give the report to the class and have the students role play with the person giving the report by asking questions.

ROMAN REPUBLIC DEVELOPED
Test

1. What is the approximate date that the Roman republic developed?

   _____

   _____

2. When the Romans broke away from the Etruscan king what form of government did they establish?

   _____

   _____

   _____

3. Who were the consuls?

   _____

   _____

4. What were the two classes of people in the Rome at this time? Describe them.

   _____

   _____

   _____

5. What eventually caused the breakup of the Roman republic?

   _____

   _____

   _____

6. What country's government was modeled after the Roman republic?

   _____

   _____

ROMAN REPUBLIC DEVELOPED
Test, Page 2

Review

1. What is the name of the early Greek alphabet developed by the Minoans?

   _____

   _____

2. From what did the Mycenaen civilization receive its name?

   _____

   _____

3. Why did God not split Israel during Solomon's reign?

   _____

   _____

4. Did the Greeks believe in the God of the Bible?

   _____

   _____

5. List in chronological order all the events studied to date.

   _____

   _____

   _____

   _____

   _____

   _____

   _____

   _____

   _____

PERSIAN WARS
Worksheet

1. What are the approximate dates of the Persian Wars?

   _____

   _____

2. What is the modern geographic area that the Persians occupied?

   _____

   _____

3. In 546 B.C. what part of Greece did the Persians conquer?

   _____

   _____

4. How did the Persian wars begin?

   _____

   _____

5. Which two Greek groups united in order to fight the Persians? Which battle did this help them to win?

   _____

   _____

   _____

6. From what did the marathon race originate?

   _____

   _____

7. Who eventually conquered the Persians?

   _____

   _____

PERSIAN WARS
Project

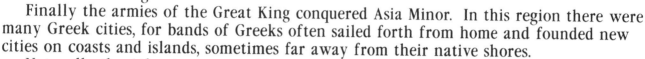

In early times a great danger threatened Greece. The Persians, a people of western Asia, were rapidly conquering all the surrounding nations. Babylon, Palestine, Phoenicia, and even Egypt were overcome by their arms. It seemed that the Great King of Persia would soon rule the world.

In some ways the Persians were a great people, but they took away from the nations which they conquered all right to think and act for themselves. How could the world make progress if everything were decided by the will of one king?

Finally the armies of the Great King conquered Asia Minor. In this region there were many Greek cities, for bands of Greeks often sailed forth from home and founded new cities on coasts and islands, sometimes far away from their native shores.

Naturally the Athenians sent soldiers and ships to aid the Greeks of Asia Minor when they rebelled against Persia. But this act so enraged the Persian king Darius that he determined to conquer Greece itself. He could not endure that those people of Europe should dare to defy him when the greatest nations of Asia trembled as his slaves. So set was he upon revenge that he ordered a slave to stand behind his throne whenever he dined and say, lest he should forget, "Master, remember the Athenians."The Great King sent messengers to Greece to order her people to submit and to send to him earth and water as a sign that he owned their land. How could the Greek cities, which did not even have a common government, refuse?

Many of the cities were terrified, and surrendered. But Sparta and Athens defied Darius. They even threw his messengers into a well and told them to take as much earth and water as they wanted. Then all the cities that stood firm formed a league to resist Persia. The Spartans were chosen leaders because they were the best soldiers.

Soon the great Persian army came. Sailing across the sea from Asia Minor, they captured all the islands and finally landed on the plain of Marathon near Athens. There were at least one hundred thousand men, and their white tents covered all the shore.

On the hills overlooking the plain were the Athenians, only about ten thousand in all. In haste they had sent to Sparta for help, but the Spartans made excuses and delayed coming. The only aid the Athenians had was from a little town called Plataea, not far away. In days past the Athenians had protected the Plataeans, and they were grateful. When the news came that Athens was in danger, every man and boy in Plataea who could carry spear and shield marched at once to join their friends. But of these brave soldiers there were only one thousand.

It seemed impossible that the Athenians should have any chance against the great Persian host. But some things not to be seen at first glance favored them. They were free men, defending their wives and little ones, while the soldiers of the Great King fought only because they were ordered to do so. It is even said that some of them had to be driven into battle with whips. The Greeks also had, better weapons. They wore bronze breastplates, and helmets with horsehair crests, while their legs were protected by bronze pieces called greaves. They bore thick, round shields, and carried long spears. Since boyhood they had exercised in gymnastics, and were strong and skillful. The weapons of the Persians were much lighter, and some of them had only armor made of wickerwork. Athens, too, had the advantage, of a brave general, Miltiades, in whom all had confidence. Though his countrymen were so few in numbers, Miltiades thought their best chance was to attack. So he drew up his warriors in a line as long as the whole front of the Persian. host, but only a few ranks deep, while the masses of the Persians seemed to fill the whole plain. Yet when he gave the signal the Greeks charged boldly down the hill. On they came, with their long line of gleaming shields, each warrior shouting the war cry, and running bravely forward.

Now with a crash the men of Asia and the men of Europe met. But in spite of their numbers both wings of the Persian army were broken, and fled. For a time their center, where the best Persian troops were stationed, stood firm, but the Athenians closed in from both sides, and soon the whole great Persian army was running to its ships.

At home in Athens, as a famous story tells, the old men and the women and children waited anxiously to hear the news. How long the time seemed! But at last they saw a runner covered with dust. He had fought that day at Marathon, and then sped over the twenty-four miles to Athens to bear the news. Exhausted, he struggled into the eager crowd. "Victory!" he gasped, and fell dead.

The Athenians were overjoyed with their success. But their leaders knew well that the Persians would come again. The wisest statesman among them, Themistocles, told them that they must be ready to fight on sea as well as on land. On his advice they built many more ships.

In spite of his rage over the defeat of his army at Marathon, King Darius was so busy with other things that he could not attack Greece again. But after his death the new king, Xerxes, took up the quarrel.

From all parts of his vast empire he collected soldiers. How many men there were in his huge army we cannot tell exactly. The Greeks thought there were over five million, and stories were told of how, wherever the multitude marched, they drank up all the pools and streams and devoured all the food, so that when they had passed the inhabitants starved to death. There were among them soldiers from forty-six nations, clad in all sorts of garments and armed with all sorts of weapons.

Xerxes assembled a great fleet, too, much larger than that of all Greece. But lest storms should hinder, he determined to lead his army by land. A great bridge of boats was therefore built across the narrow strait between Asia Minor and Europe, and over this the long procession marched while the Great King watched from a marble throne. Then they journeyed southward to, assail Greece, while the fleet, sailing along the coast, kept as nearly even with them as possible. All Greece was terrified, and some of the cities sent messengers to Xerxes, begging to be spared from destruction. But there were still brave hearts in Sparta and Athens. In northern Greece, between steep mountains and the sea, is a narrow pass

PLAN OF BATTLE OF MARATHON

called Thermopylae, the "Hot Gates," because there was a spring of warm water. Through this the Persian host must march. But in this pass were three hundred Spartans led by one of their kings, Leonidas, with a number of allies from other cities.

The Spartans seemed a mere handful of men against so many Persian soldiers, and Xerxes contemptuously ordered the Greeks to give up their arms. "Come and take them," replied Leonidas. Only a few Persians could enter the pass at one time; again and again they tried, but were always hurled back by the brave Spartans. Even Xerxes' best troops were beaten. For two days Leonidas hold the pass.

Finally a traitor Greek told the Persians of a path over the hills by which they might fall upon the Spartans from the rear. For the Greeks to stay in the pass longer was certain death. But by a law of Sparta her warriors must never flee. Leonidas and his three hundred felt they could not desert their post. Struck by their brave example, many of the allies said they would stay, too.

So Leonidas and his men held their ground and fought till every man perished. But heaps upon heaps of slain Persians proved how bravely they had struggled. The pass of Thermopylae was lost, but the world can never forget the example of Leonidas and his

PERSIAN WARS
Project, Page 3

three hundred. Of such stuff were Spartans made.

In later days a monument was built to mark the place where the heroes died. Upon it were carved no high-sounding words of praise, but a simple verse which meant a great deal more:

"Go, passerby, to Sparta tell
Obedient to her law we fell."

The Persians now marched on and overran northern Greece. Even Athens could not be defended. But her people were still unconquered. Led by the clever Themistocles, they embarked upon the ships which they had so wisely built. The women and children were taken to a place of safety, but the men again put to sea. Though the Persians captured the city and ruthlessly destroyed the buildings, they had not destroyed the real Athens. Athens was in the fleet, still eager to strike a blow for freedom. The other Greeks now wanted to sail away to defend their own homes, but Themistocles felt it was better to fight the fleet of Xerxes at once. So, pretending to be a secret friend to the Persians, he sent a message to their king telling him that the Greeks were quarreling among themselves and that if he would send vessels to close up the entrance to the bay where their ships lay, he could easily destroy them.

Xerxes did so, and the next day he had a lofty throne set up on a hill overlooking the sea that he might watch his ships overcome the Greeks. Since he had three times as many vessels, he felt sure that he would win. In the blue Bay of Salamis the great battle took place. Driven by their long oars, ship dashed against ship, each striving to crash into the other with her sharp beak. The air was filled with arrows and darts, and above the din rose the fierce shouts of the warriors. Sometimes the ships came side by side, and the men swarmed over the rails to fight it out hand to hand. But the Greeks were the better sailors, and, moreover, were thinking of their wives and little ones, whom they must save from the enemy. When the battle was over the vast Persian fleet had been beaten and many of its vessels sunk. Xerxes had still a large army and many ships left.

But his heart failed him. He knew now what manner of men the Greeks were. So he returned to Asia, leaving behind merely a part of his army to carry on the war. These soldiers the Greeks overcame the next year in another great land battle. Thus Greece was saved. The Persian king might still tyrannize over the people of Asia, but Europe was to be free. Had the Greeks been frightened by mere numbers, all would have been lost. But Marathon and Salamis showed the world what a few brave men, who prefer death to slavery, can do.

Persian Wars
Project 2

The Greek Trireme
Materials

One copy of the ship on the following page (per child)

One sheet of white construction paper (per child)

Blue tissue paper (several shades)

Markers

Scissors

Glue

Paint brush

Instructions

1. Color the ship and cut out.

2. Tear tissue paper into one inch squares.

3. Mix glue and water in equal portions.

4. Orient the paper horizontally and brush glue mixture onto bottom half of construction paper.

5. Place torn blue paper onto construction paper where glue mixture has been applied.

6. Brush over the top of the blue paper to secure it.

7. Glue ship onto the "blue sea" created with the tissue paper.

The Greek Trireme

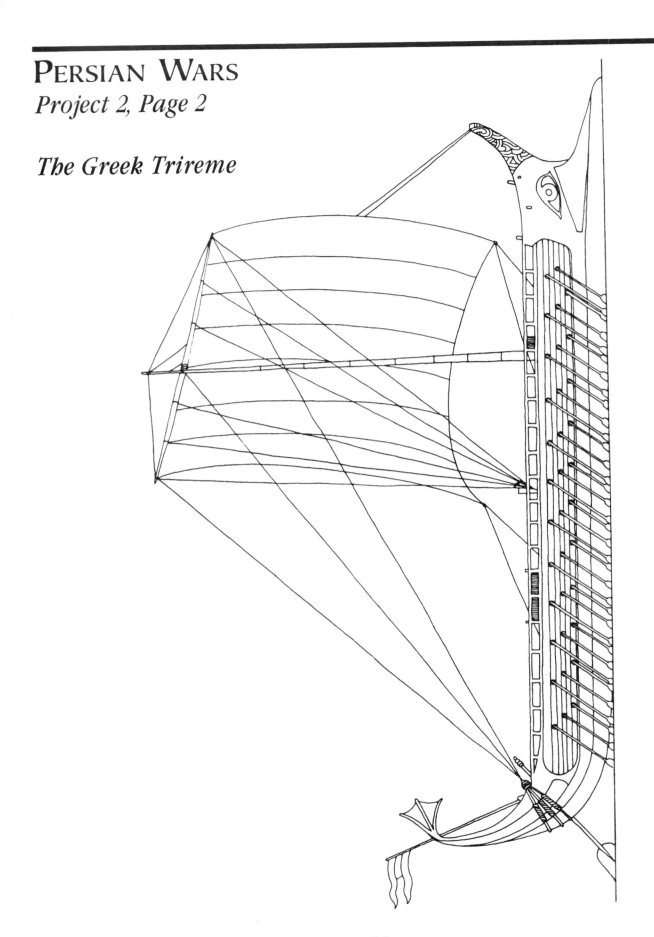

PERSIAN WARS
Test

1. What were the approximate dates of the Persian Wars?

_____

_____

2. How did the Persian Wars begin? Which countries were involved in the Persian Wars?

_____

_____

_____

3. Who won the Battle of Marathon? What modern day event evolved from this battle?
   How did this occur?

_____

_____

_____

_____

4. When did the Persian empire begin to decline?

_____

_____

_____

5. Who eventually conquered the Persians?

_____

_____

_____

PERSIAN WARS
Test, Page 2

Review

1. Did the Greeks believe in the God of the Bible?

   _____

   _____

2. What was the purpose of the Olympics?

   _____

   _____

3. Who are Romulus and Remus? What do they have to do with Rome?

   _____

   _____

   _____

4. What is the Scripture reference for the fall of Israel and Judah?

   _____

   _____

5. List in chronological order the events studied to date.

   _____

   _____

   _____

   _____

   _____

   _____

   _____

   _____

PERICLES AND THE PELOPONNESIAN WAR
Worksheet

1. What are the approximate dates for Pericles and the Peloponnesian War?

   _____

   _____

2. When the Persian wars ended what *period* did Athens enter?

   _____

   _____

3. Name three things that occurred during the *Golden Age?*

   _____

   _____

   _____

4. Where does western civilization find its roots?

   _____

   _____

5. Who was the most famous politician during Greece's *Golden Age?*

   _____

   _____

6. Describe the *Delian League.*

   _____

   _____

   _____

   _____

PERICLES AND THE PELOPONNESIAN WAR
Worksheet, Page 2

7. As the city of Athens became more influential what city became threatened?

   _____

   _____

8. In 431 Corinth and Corcyra became enemies. Sparta supported Corinth and Athens supported Corcyra. What event did this cause? How long did this event last? What were the results?

   _____

   _____

   _____

   _____

   _____

   _____

   _____

PERICLES AND THE PELOPONNESIAN WAR
Project

Newspaper Article

Using the card and the resources on the card use the following pages to have students write a newspaper article for the Athenian Chronicle or the Spartan Gazette. Suggest to your students that they write about something they find particularly interesting about the Peloponnesian War. Point out to them that depending on which paper they write for will depend on who they are supporting, Corinth or Corcyra. After the articles are written you may want to compile them into two papers to share with the entire class.

(As an aside you may want to include some of the articles in your school's newsletter.)

A Greek soldier saying farewell to his wife and parents

ATHENIAN CHRONICLE

SPARTAN GAZETTE

PERICLES AND THE PELOPONNESIAN WAR
Test

1. What is another name for the Classical Period in Greece?

   _____

   _____

2. Finish the sentences below as they relate to the Classical Period in Greece, especially in

   Athens.   The city became _____ and was a center for the _____.

   The Greek idea that _____ is the measure of _____ things reached its

   _____ during this period. _____ civilization finds its _____

   in Greek culture and particularly in this Golden Age.

3. Who was Pericles?

   _____

   _____

4. As Athenians influence began to increase, how did the Spartans begin to feel?

   _____

   _____

   _____

5. What was the Delian League? Why did it form?

   _____

   _____

6. What was the cause of the Peloponnesian War? Who did Athens support?

   Who did Sparta support?

   _____

   _____

7. How long did the Peloponnesian War last? Who eventually won?

   _____

   _____

PERICLES AND THE PELOPONNESIAN WAR
Test, Page 2

Review

1. Who were the first citizens of Rome?

2. Describe how the colonization of Greece began. Where did the colonies develop?

3. To what nation did Israel fall? To what nation did Judah fall?

4. What was God's purpose in sending His prophets to His people?

5. List in chronological order all the events studied to date.

GREEK PHILOSOPHERS
Worksheet

1. What are the approximate dates of the Greek Philosophers?

_____

_____

2. How did the early Greek people answer questions of how the world works?

_____

_____

3. For what were the Greek philosophers known?

_____

_____

_____

4. What is the Socratic Method? Who invented it?

_____

_____

_____

5. What is Sophistry?

_____

_____

_____

6. How did Socrates die?

_____

_____

_____

_____

GREEK PHILOSOPHERS
Worksheet, Page 2

7. Who was a famous student of Socrates? What kind of school did he start?

_____

_____

_____

8. Who was Aristotle? For what was he known?

_____

_____

_____

9. What did the Stoics believe?

_____

_____

_____

_____

10. What did the Epicurians believe?

_____

_____

_____

_____

GREEK PHILOSOPHERS
Project

Two Philosophers, Socrates and Plato

About a century before the Age of Pericles, someone asked a very wise man, "What is a philosopher?" He replied, "At the games, some try to win glory, some buy and sell for money, and some watch what others do. So it is in life; and philosophers are those who watch, who study nature, and search for wisdom." Now during the time of Pericles a young man lived in Athens who was to become famous as a philosopher, though perhaps no one thought so at the time. His father was a sculptor. The son followed the same occupation, and probably worked with hammer and chisel upon some of the statues that made Athens beautiful.

This young man, whose name was Socrates, studied with some of the teachers of the time; but he was not satisfied with their teachings and he made up his mind that the best way for him to find out what was true was to think for himself. One of the conclusions was that, as the gods needed nothing, so the man who needed least was in that respect most like them. Therefore he trained himself to live on coarse and scanty food, he learned to bear heat and cold, and even when he served in the army and had to march over ice and snow, he did not give up his habit of going barefooted.

Socrates was not handsome. He had a flat nose, thick lips, and prominent eyes. He became bald early in life. He walked awkwardly, and used to astonish people by sometimes standing still for hours when he wanted to think out something. On the other hand, he had a beautiful voice, he grew bright and witty and brave and kindhearted. As he grew older, he used to spend the whole day wherever people were to be found. He went to the market place, to the workshops, and to the porticoes where the Athenians were accustomed to walk up and down and talk together. He was ready to talk with anyone, rich or poor, old or young, and to teach them what he believed to be right and true. His way of doing this was by asking questions and so making them think for themselves. For instance, his pupil Plato represents him as having a talk with a boy named Lysis. "Of course your father and mother love you and wish you to be happy?" he asked. "Certainly," replied the boy. "Is a slave happy, who is not allowed to do what he likes?" "No." "Then your parents, wishing you to be happy, let you do as you choose? Would your father let you drive his chariot in a race?" "Surely not," said Lysis. "But he lets a hired servant drive it and even pays him for so doing," Socrates continued. "Does he care more for this man than for you?" "No, he does not." "As your mother wishes you to be happy, of course she lets you do as you like when you are with her, " said the philosopher. "She never hinders you from touching her loom or shuttle when she is weaving, does she?" Lysis laughed and replied, "She not only hinders me, but I should be beaten if I touched them." "When you take the lyre, do your parents hinder you from tightening and loosening any string that you please? How is this?" "I think it is because I know the one, but not the other," the boy replied thoughtfully. "So it is," said Socrates, "and all persons will trust us in those things wherein they have found us wise."

This was the philosopher's manner of teaching an honest boy; but if a man was not sincere, Socrates would tangle him up with questions until the man had said that sickness and health, right and wrong, and black and white were the same things. He prayed and offered sacrifices to the gods as the laws required; but he believed that there was one god over all, and that to be honest and good was better than sacrifices. He taught his followers to say this prayer: "Father Jupiter, give us all good, whether we ask it or not; and avert from us all evil, though we do not pray thee so to do. Bless all our good actions, and reward them with success and happiness."

Socrates had made many enemies. The rulers hated him because he declared, among other remarks of the sort, that to govern a state was far more difficult than to steer a vessel; but that, although no one would attempt to steer a vessel without training, every one thought himself fit to govern a state. He was accused of preaching new gods and of giving false teaching to the young and was condemned to die. He was perfectly calm and serene. He told his judges that it was a gain to die; but that it was unjust for them to put him to death, and therefore they would suffer for it. He would not allow his family to come before them to plead for his life, and he would not escape when his friends offered to open the way.

It was thirty days from the time that he was sentenced until his death. He spent much of this time in talking with his pupils. One of those whom he loved best was Plato; and Plato afterwards wrote an account of the last days of his master. Socrates said that his death was only going "to some happy state of the blessed." He was asked in what manner he wished to be buried; and he replied with a smile, "Just as you please, if only you catch me."

He was to die by poison. When the cup was brought, he drank it as calmly as if it had been wine, he comforted his disciples, who were weeping around him. At last, he called to one of the young men, "Crito, we owe a cock to Aesculapius; pay it, therefore, and do not neglect it." Aesculapius was the god to whom a man who was grateful for his recovery from illness made a sacrifice; and Socrates was so sure of a happier life to come that he felt as if death was passing from sickness to health. It is no wonder that his pupil Plato said, "This man was the best of all of his time that we have known, and, moreover, the most wise and just."

After the death of Socrates, Plato traveled from one country to another. He studied the people, the laws, and the customs. If there were philosophers in the land, he learned all that he could from them. "Plato, how long do you intend to remain a student?" one of his

GREEK PHILOSOPHERS
Project, Page 3

friends asked. He replied, "As long as I am not ashamed to grow wiser and better." In the course of his travels, he went to Syracuse, on the island of Sicily. The ruler of Syracuse was Dionysius. He was called a tyrant, which meant that he had seized the throne unlawfully. Dionysius himself wrote poems, and he was always glad to welcome philosophers and scholars to his court. Unluckily, he and Plato fell into an argument. Plato not only got the better of it, but dared to make some bold remarks about tyrants. Dionysius was so angry that he came near putting his honored guest to death. He did bribe some one to sell the philosopher as a slave on his homeward journey. This was done, but Plato's friends bought back his freedom.

At length Plato returned to Athens. A little way outside of the city was a large public garden or park, along the Cephissus River. Here grew plane trees and olive trees. Here were temples and statues. This was called the Academy, in honor of one Academus, who had left it to the city for gymnastics. Plato's father seems to have owned a piece of land near this park; and here Plato opened a school for all who chose to become learners. It took its name from the park known as the Academy. The most brilliant young men of the time were eager to come to the Academy to study with Plato. He discussed difficult questions with his students and he wrote on the deepest subjects, but with so much humor and sweetness that many people fancied him to be descended from Apollo, the god of eloquence. Long afterwards, Cicero the greatest Roman orator, declared that if Jupiter were to speak Greek, he would use the language of Plato.

One of Plato's sayings was, "To conquer one's self is the highest wisdom." He not only taught self-control, but he practiced it. A friend came upon him one day unexpectedly and asked why he was holding his arm up as if to strike. "I am punishing a passionate man,"

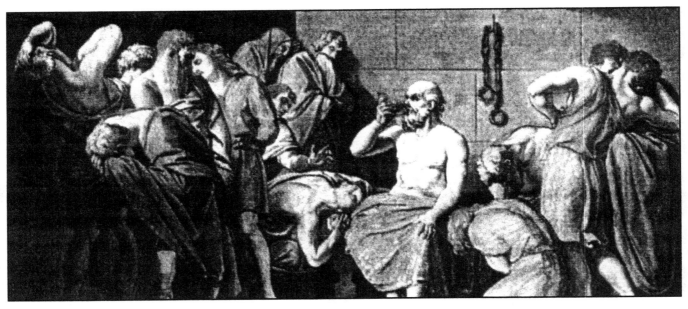

Project, Page 4

Plato replied. It seemed that he had raised his arm to strike a disobedient slave; but had stopped because he found himself in a passion. Even when he was told that his enemies were spreading false stories about him, he did not fly into a fit of anger; he only said quietly, "I will live so that none will believe them." He was simple and friendly in his manner. There is a tradition that some strangers who met him at the Olympian games were so pleased with him that they gladly accepted his invitation to visit him in Athens. When their visit was near its end, they said, "But will you not introduce us to your famous namesake, the philosopher Plato?" They were greatly surprised when their host replied quietly, "I am the person whom you wish to see."

When Plato died, he was buried in his garden. His followers raised altars and statues in his memory, and for many years the day of his birth was celebrated among them with rejoicing.

Discussion

1. What is a philosopher?

2. Describe the physical attributes of Socrates?

3. How did Socrates teach his students?

4. How did Socrates die?

5. How did Plato continue in Socrates' tradition?

6. What did Plato believe about self-control?

7. Were Socrates and Plato teaching "Biblical Truth?"

GREEK PHILOSOPHERS
Project 2

Finish the sentences below using *The Usborne Illustrated History, The Greeks,* page 79.

SOCRATES thought that people would behave well if

_____.

He challenged people to think about _____

_____.

He became very popular with some _____.

They charged him with _____ and he was forced to _____

himself.

PLATO reported _____ ideas because he never wrote them down. In his

own work, Plato tried to find _____

and set out detailed rules of how this could be done.

ARISTOTLE was born in _____ and was a pupil of _____. He had a

wide knowledge of _____ and _____. Aristotle was interest in

_____ and _____, and finding the ideal way to run a _____

_____. One of his pupils was _____.

GREEK PHILOSOPHERS
Project 3

The instructions for this project can be found on Appendix 2-1.

The Sophists and the Philosophers

I

In ancient Athens, it was very important for a man to be able to speak persuasively. That's because almost every important decision in Athens, from whether or not they would go to war to whether a man would be punished for a crime was decided by an assembly of free men. If an issue was important to him, or if someone accused him of wrongdoing, he had to speak persuasively for his own cause. Because of this, it is not surprising that rhetoric, the art of teaching persuasively, was the subject that the Athenians were most interested in as the core of their education. A group of men known as "the Sophists", or "wise ones", became famous for their ability to, among other things, teach young men to persuade others. The problem was that the Sophists couldn't care less about whether what was being argued for was true or false, but only about whether the argument was persuasive.

II

One man didn't approve of this sort of thinking at all! His name was Socrates and he was quite willing to step on other's toes in his quest for the truth. He didn't care if his arguments didn't sound pretty, only if they came closer to the truth. To find the truth, he just kept asking questions. And then he would question the questions. Though he didn't participate in politics himself, he was even willing to question the ways in which the Athenians had governed themselves for years. He asked so many questions that the people eventually decided that he was a threat to the state and put him on trial. Uncompromising to the end, Socrates gave a defense speech that insulted his audience. Unsurprisingly, he was convicted and forced to drink poison.

GREEK PHILOSOPHERS
Project 3, Page 2

Vocabulary

1. *persuasively:*
   _____

   _____

2. *assembly:*
   _____

   _____

3. *core:*
   _____

   _____

4. *argument:*
   _____

   _____

5. *rhetoric:*
   _____

   _____

6. *quest:*
   _____

   _____

7. *uncompromising:*
   _____

   _____

8. *insulted:*
   _____

   _____

9. *convicted:*
   _____

   _____

GREEK PHILOSOPHERS
Project 3, Page 2

Key Word Outline

I _____

1 _____

2 _____

3 _____

4 _____

5 _____

6 _____

II _____

1 _____

2 _____

3 _____

4 _____

5 _____

6 _____

7 _____

8 _____

GREEK PHILOSOPHERS
Project 3, Page 3

Answers
Vocabulary
1. *persuasively:* convincingly
2. *assembly:* gathering
3. *core:* the heart, most important part
4. *argument:* a rational attempt to convince
5. *rhetoric:* the art of persuasive speaking
6. *quest:* search
7. *uncompromising:* unwilling to give in or change at all
8. *insulted:* said bad things about
9. *convicted:* declared guilty

Key Word Outline
I. The Sophists and the Art of Rhetoric
1. Important, speak, persuasively
2. Decision, decided, assembly
3. Speak, own, cause
4. Rhetoric, core, education
5. Sophists, famous, teach
6. Problem, care, truth

II. Socrates and the Search for Truth
1. One, didn't, approve
2. Socrates, question, truth
3. Find, asking, questions
4. Question, questions
5. Question, Athenians, governed
6. Decided, threat, trial
7. Defense, Speech, insulted
8. Convicted, drink, poison

GREEK PHILOSOPHERS
Test

1. What are the approximate dates for the Greek Philosophers?

   _____

   _____

2. Why did the Greeks tell stories about the gods?

   _____

   _____

   _____

3. For what were philosophers around 450 B.C. known?

   _____

   _____

4. Place the following three names in chronological order: Plato, Aristotle, and Socrates.

   _____

   _____

5. What was the *Socratic method?*

   _____

   _____

6. Define sophistry.

   _____

   _____

7. Why and how was Socrates executed?

   _____

   _____

   _____

8. Who was Socrates' most famous student? What did he establish?

_____

_____

_____

9. For what was Aristotle known? Who was his teacher?

_____

_____

_____

10. What did the Stoics and Epicurians believe?

_____

_____

_____

Review

1. Name three prophets.

_____

_____

2. Where does today's democracy find its roots?

_____

_____

3. How did the Persian wars begin?

_____

_____

4. How did the name "Phoenicians" develop?

_____

_____

_____

5. List in chronological order all the events studied to date.

_____

_____

_____

_____

_____

_____

_____

_____

_____

_____

_____

_____

NEHEMIAH AND THE JEWISH RETURN
Worksheet

1. What was the approximate date of Nehemiah and the Jewish Return?

   _____

   _____

2. What was Nehemiah's profession?

   _____

   _____

3. Who led the initial return of the exiles back to Israel?

   _____

   _____

4. Ten years after this initial return who led another group of exiles back to Israel?

   _____

   _____

5. In all likelihood the queen in the first chapter of Nehemiah was _____,

   to whom Nehemiah was a _____.

6. Why did Nehemiah wish to return to his homeland of Jerusalem?

   _____

   _____

   _____

   _____

   _____

NEHEMIAH AND THE JEWISH RETURN
Worksheet, Page 2

7. Who was Nehemiah concerned about supporting his desire to return to Jerusalem?
   What did Nehemiah do because of his concern?

   _____

   _____

   _____

8. What was the kings response to Nehemiah?

   _____

   _____

9. What did Nehemiah and his fellow Jews
   build in only 52 days?

   _____

   _____

   _____

   _____

NEHEMIAH AND THE JEWISH RETURN
Project

Map Excercise

Among the Jewish captives who were carried into Shushan (Persia) was a young girl by the name of Ester. Because she found favor in the sight of the king, she was made queen. When the lives of the Jews in this country were endangered, she interceded with King Ahasuerus and was able to save them.

After many years of captivity, Zerubbabel received permission from King Cyrus to lead a company back to Jerusalem, where they began the rebuilding of the Temple. Enemies hindered the building, and God sent the prophets Haggai and Zechariah to encourage the people to complete the Temple.

Ezra, a devout Jew of the Captivity, went up from Babylon to Jerusalem and taught the people of the law.

Nehemiah, cupbearer to King Artaxerxes, upon hearing that the walls of Jerusalem had been broken down and the gates burned with fire, asked for permission to go up to Jerusalem and encourage his people to repair the walls. His request was granted and he went. The work of rebuilding the walls was hindered by Sanballat and a company of opposers, who made sport of their attempts. However, Nehemiah persisted and the walls were completed.

Trace Nehemiah's journey to Jerusalem on the map below.

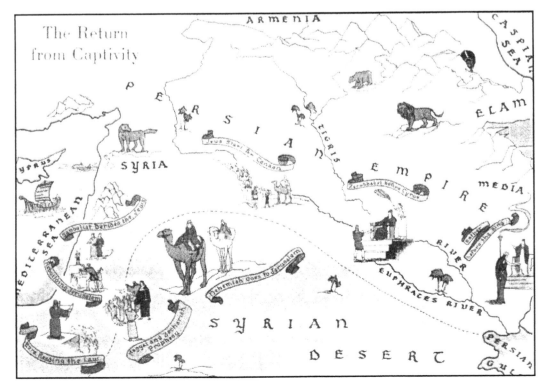

NEHEMIAH AND THE JEWISH RETURN

Test

1. Who was Nehemiah?

_____

_____

2. Why did he want to return to his homeland of Jerusalem?

_____

_____

3. Who was Nehemiah afraid might not support his decision to return to Jerusalem?

_____

_____

4. What was the above person's response to Nehemiah? Why?

_____

_____

5. How many days did it take for Nehemiah and his fellow Jews to rebuild the wall around Jerusalem?

_____

_____

6. What is the approximate date of Nehemiah and the Jewish Return?

_____

_____

Review

1. When the Romans broke away from the Etruscan king what form of government did they establish?

_____

_____

NEHEMIAH AND THE JEWISH RETURN
Test, Page 2

2. How did the Persian wars begin?

_____

_____

3. What was the first European civilization? Where did it develop?

_____

_____

_____

4. What was found at Athens and Thebes that has aided our understanding of the Myceneans?

_____

_____

5. List in chronological order all the events studied to date. Next to each one write the appropriate date.

_____

_____

_____

_____

_____

_____

_____

_____

_____

_____

ALEXANDER THE GREAT
Worksheet

1. What are the dates for Alexander the Great?

   _____

   _____

2. Who was Alexander the Great's father?

   _____

   _____

3. Who was Alexander's teacher?

   _____

   _____

4. When did Alexander become the ruler of Greece?

   _____

   _____

5. Alexander was a _____ genius. He invaded
   Persia in _____ and soon gained
   control of _____ _____.
   Next, he conquered _____, and in
   _____ he defeated the Persian king,
   _____. This victory positioned
   him to rule all of _____. He wanted to
   build a huge _____. In fact, he
   wanted to _____ all of the known
   _____. He desired the _____
   to be under _____.

ALEXANDER THE GREAT
Worksheet, Page 2

6. Why was he called Alexander the "Great"?

_____

_____

7. After his death who came to rule his kingdom?

_____

_____

_____

8. In comparing Alexander's life with the life of Christ what do we see?

_____

_____

_____

_____

_____

_____

_____

_____

_____

ALEXANDER THE GREAT
Project

King Philip of Macedonia, had a son by the name of Alexander. If the stories of his boyhood are true, he must have been a remarkable even as a small boy. When he was only a child, some ambassadors from Persia came to the court of Macedonia. Philip was away, and they were received by the little prince. Imagine their surprise when the child began to ask the kind of questions about their country that a grown man and sovereign would have been likely to ask. He wanted to know about the roads and the distances between places. "What sort of man is your king?" he questioned. "How does he treat his enemies? Why is Persia strong? Is it because she has much gold or a large army?" It is no wonder that the ambassadors gazed at him and then looked at each other in amazement, for they had never before seen a prince like this one. Another story that is told of the boy is of his taming the horse Bucephalus. It was so vicious that the grooms could do nothing with it, and Philip angrily ordered it taken away. The boy Alexander cried, "What a horse they are losing for want of skill and spirit to manage him!" "Young man" retorted his father, "you find fault with your elders as if you could manage the horse better." "And I certainly could," the boy declared bodly. The king forgot his anger and said, "If you fail, what forfeit will you pay?" "The price of the horse," replied the boy stoutly. Everybody laughed; but Alexander was neither boasting nor jesting. He had noticed something that not one of the others had marked, namely, that the horse was annoyed by his own shadow, which was constantly moving before him. He took firm hold of the bridle and turned the horse toward the sun, he spoke gently and stroked him with his hand, then he leaped upon his back. He let the horse gallop about as much as he chose, then he rode quietly up to his father. Philip did not laugh at him then, but kissed him and said, "Seek another empire, my son, for that which I shall leave you is not worthy of you." Philip saw that a boy like Alexander would not be satisfied with any ordinary

teachers, and he asked Aristotle, a famous philosopher who had long been a pupil of Plato, to come to his court to instruct his son. For a schoolroom, Philip gave them a large garden with many trees and shady, winding paths, much like Plato's garden on the Cephissus. Alexander was an eager student. He wanted to learn everything, but he was especially fond of the Iliad. When he was sixteen, Philip went to war and left his son in charge of the kingdom. One of the subject tribes thought this was an excellent time to rebel; but the young regent called out his troops, drove the tribe out of their city, filled the place with new settlers, and gave it the name of Alexandropolis. Alexander was only twenty years old when Philip died. "Now is the time to free ourselves from Macedonia," thought a tribe of wild mountaineers. So thought also Demosthenes and the Greeks. But "the boy," as Demosthenes called him, first marched against the mountaineers, then against Greece, and conquered both. The mountaineers had heavy wagons loaded with stone ready to roll down upon Alexander and his men in a narrow pass through which they would have to advance. The quick-witted young commander bade his men lie down on the ground with their shields over their heads. The wagons rolled over them as over a well-paved road. Greece, too, was promptly subdued. The young ruler was a very wise man. He was bent upon conquering Persia, and he asked the Greeks to help him. Even though they themselves had been overcome by the Macedonian, they were ready to march against their old enemy, the Persians, with so excellent a general as leader. He was more sensible than Xerxes, for he did not make the mistake of taking an army too large to feed and move; but the thirty-five or thirty-eight thousand men whom he did take were perfectly trained and finely equipped. Alexander was mounted on Bucephalus, the very horse that he had tamed a few years earlier. He led his troops across the Hellespont; and now for the moment he was not a soldier, but an earnest lover of real poetry; and he went first of all to visit Troy. There he offered up sacrifices to Athene and to the spirits of the heroes of the Trojan War. He hung a wreath on the pillar of Achilles's tomb, for he had persuaded himself long before this that he was descended from the Grecian hero. Darius III, king of Persia, knew of course what this bold young man was attempting; and not far from the Hellespont, his troops were drawn up on the bank of a little river called Granicus. "It is unlucky to begin war in the month Daisius " (June), said the Macedonian officers to Alexander. "I have changed its name," declared their king; "it is no longer Daisius, but the Second Artemisius " (May). They thought it too late in the day to cross; but Alexander plunged into the river, and the troops followed the two white plumes on his crest. The water was rough, the banks were slimy, and at the top were the masses of Persians, drawn up in line of battle; but Alexander won the day. He was generous with the spoils. He had brazen statues made of the men who had fallen, he gave lavish gifts to the Greeks, especially to the Athenians, and he sent home to his mother the purple hangings and the gold and silver dishes found in the tents of the Persians. Alexander marched on into Phrygia, taking cities as he went. In Gordium he went to see the famous "Gordian knot," made of cords cut from the bark of a tree. There was an ancient prophecy that he who could untie it would conquer the world. Alexander drew his sword and cut it. Then he moved on in a zigzag course from city to city. At Issus, he met the Persian forces again. It did not seem possible for them to learn that too many men in a narrow plain were worse than too few; and soon the Persian king and his troops were fleeing for their lives. In the tent of Darius there were quantities of gold and silver and the richest of furnishings. Alexander amused himself by looking at the bath of the Persian monarch with its golden basins, vials, boxes, and vases, and by smelling of the various perfumes. Then he said to his friends, "It seems that to be a king was this!" He was far more interested in a beautiful golden casket that came from the spoils of the Persians. "Darius," he said, "used to keep his ointments in this casket; but I, who have no time to anoint myself, will convert it to a nobler use"; and in it he laid the copy of the Iliad which he was accustomed to place under his pillow when he slept. After the Macedonian rule was well established in Asia Minor, Alexander set out for Egypt. His welcome in Egypt was somewhat different from that which he had received at the Granicus; for the Egyptians had been conquered by the Persians, and they were delighted with the hope of being free from Persian rule. Near the mouth of the Nile he noticed a broad tongue of land with a lake on one side and a deep, wide harbor on the other. "That is an excellent site for a city," he said, and he ordered the walls to be marked out at once. The soil was black, and the lines were marked out by sprinkling flour. These lines curved around the harbor, and from their ends straight lines were drawn to the shore. Alexander was pleased to see that the figure was in the shape of a Macedonian cloak. So it was that the city of Alexandria was founded. After the battle of Issus, the wife and daughter of Darius had been captured. Darius now wrote to Alexander, offering him ten thousand talents, all the lands west of the Euphrates, and the hand of his daughter in marriage, if he would make a treaty of friendship with him. Parmenio, one of the Macedonian generals, said, "If I were Alexander, I would accept this." "So would I, "said Alexander, "if I were Parmenio." He had treated Darius's family with the utmost courtesy and kindness, but about this time the queen was taken ill and died. He gave her a most magnificent funeral. When Darius heard of it, he prayed to the gods that if his kingdom must fall, none but Alexander should sit upon its throne.

Darius brought together all his forces, elephants, war-chariots with sharp swords stretching out from the yoke and the hubs of the wheels, and thousands upon thousands of men from wherever he could get them. He even hired some soldiers from Greece. A terrible battle was fought at Arbela, and Alexander was the victor. This battle decided the question who should rule Persia. At the capitals of the kingdom, Babylon and Susa, Alexander found enormous amounts of money. What he wanted, however, was to capture the Persian king; but there was a conspiracy among Darius's generals, and he was slain by his own men. "Tell Alexander I gave him my hand," said Darius to a Macedonian soldier who found him where his men had left him for dead. Alexander had conquered Persia. He had more power and more wealth than any one man had ever held before; but he cared less for power and wealth than for the pleasure of getting them. He seemed to be seized with a perfect frenzy for conquest. He pushed on and on, north, south, north again, then south to the mouth of the Indus, conquering as he marched. Wherever he went, he founded cities. Eighteen of them he named for himself, and one for Bucephalus. He planned to conquer Arabia, then, turning westward, to overpower northern Africa, Italy, and Spain; in short to become ruler of the whole world. He returned to Babylon to meet fresh troops. Suddenly he was taken ill and died. No one could govern such an empire, and after many years of fighting it was divided into three parts, to be ruled by three of his generals. The new empire of Rome was growing up in the West and Alexander's conquests in Asia finally fell into Roman hands.

After reading the above text about Alexander the Great examine the map on the following page to see the vast geographic area spanning many kingdoms which he conquered in his brief lifetime.

Discuss with your teacher the incredible empire he had conquered and note what the means of transportation and communication were at this time to help fathom the tremendous feat he had accomplished.

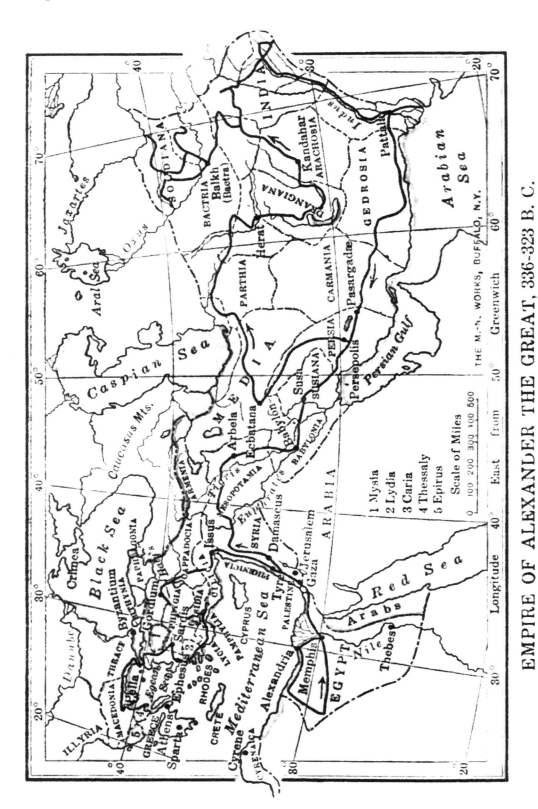

EMPIRE OF ALEXANDER THE GREAT, 336-323 B. C.

ALEXANDER THE GREAT
Project 2

The instructions for this project can be found on Appendix 2-1.

Alexander and the Dream of Greek Unity

I

The Greeks were very good soldiers and sailors. They proved this when they defeated two different invasions by the vast and mighty Persian Empire. In fact, the Persian emperor loved to hire them as mercenaries whenever he could. The problem was that because the Greeks were divided up into all sorts of little city-states that were constantly fighting among each other. The Peloponnesian War was the greatest, but not the last, of these many wars. Many Greeks believed that if they could all get together into one big nation, they could conquer the Persian Empire and maybe even the whole known world. The problem was that no one really seemed to know how to bring this about.

II

One man had his ideas. His name was Phillip and he was the king of Macedon, a region just north of Greece. He would either conquer or ally himself with all of the little city-states, and then lead them all on a "crusade of revenge" against Persia. He had a tough time subduing the cities of Athens and Thebes, particularly when Athens' democracy was under the sway of the great orator Demosthenes. Not long after Phillip had finally made himself the master of all of Greece he was assassinated, though we don't know by whom.

III

When his young son Alexander came to the throne, many thought he was too young to continue his father's achievements, and took advantage of the opportunity to rebel. That was a bad mistake. Young Alexander reacted swiftly and brutally to crush the revolt, and he even wiped the city of Thebes out completely and sold its inhabitants into slavery! With the rest of Greece afraid to revolt again, he felt safe to carry on his father's dream of invading Persia. With an amazing campaign he then conquered the entire Persian Empire, including Egypt, and even western India! Unfortunately for the empire, however, Alexander died while he was very young and the Macedonian leaders couldn't decide on who should be the next king. Eventually, Alexander's generals divided the empire into several parts which became known as the "Hellenistic" (or Greek) kingdoms. Each was named after the dynasty, or ruling family, that ruled in them. After a whole generation of warfare, three main Hellenistic kingdoms emerged. They were the Ptolemaic Kingdom in Egypt, the Seleucid Kingdom in Syria and Mesopotamia and the Antigonid Kingdom in Macedonia. When Alexander died, the dream of Greek unity had never been so close to success and never would until the end of the Roman Empire.

ALEXANDER THE GREAT
Project 2, Page 2

Key Word Outline

I _____

  1 _____

  2 _____

  3 _____

  4 _____

  5 _____

  6 _____

  7 _____

II _____

  1 _____

  2 _____

  3 _____

  4 _____

  5 _____

III _____

  1 _____

  2 _____

  3 _____

  4 _____

  5 _____

  6 _____

ALEXANDER THE GREAT
Project 2, Page 3

7 _____

8 _____

9 _____

Vocabulary

1. *empire:*

2. *mercenaries:*

3. *ally:*

4. *crusade:*

5. *subduing:*

6. *sway:*

7. *orator:*

8. *assassinated:*

9. *hellenistic:*

ALEXANDER THE GREAT
Project 2, Page 4

Vocabulary

1. *empire:* a large territory ruled by one man or a collection of nations ruled by one nation
2. *mercenaries:* men who fight for hire
3. *ally:* one who fights alongside
4. *crusade:* a war based on religious or moral indignation
5. *subduing:* forcing to do one's will
6. *sway:* to bring to one's own side in a conflict or disagreement
7. *orator:* one known for public speaking
8. *assassinated:* deliberately killed; usually reserved for the killing of public men
9. *hellenistic:* Greek in culture

Key Word Outline

I. The Greek Dilemma
1. Greeks, good, soldiers
2. Proved, defeated, Persian Empire
3. Persians, hire, mercenaries
4. Problem, divided, fighting
5. Pelopennesian War, example
6. Many, believed, conquer
7. No one, seemed, know

II. Phillip's Plan
1. One, man, ideas
2. Phillips, king, Macedon
3. Conquer, ally, lead
4. Subduing, Athens, Thebes
5. After, master, assassinated

III. Alexander's Triumph
1. Alexander, opportunity, rebel
2. Brutally, crush, Thebes
3. Safe, carry on, dream
4. Amazing, campaign, conquered
5. Unfortunately, died, young
6. Generals, divided, empire
7. Warfare, three, emerged
8. Ptolemaic, Seleucid, Antigonid
9. Never, so, close

ALEXANDER THE GREAT
Test

1. What are the dates for Alexander the Great?

   _____

   _____

2. Who was Alexander the Great's father?

   _____

   _____

3. When did Alexander become ruler of Greece?

   _____

   _____

4. What was Alexander's greatest desire? How did he accomplish this?

   _____

   _____

   _____

5. Why was he called Alexander the "Great?"

   _____

   _____

6. Who took control of Greece after Alexander's death?

   _____

   _____

Review

1. What is the Socratic method?

   _____

   _____

ALEXANDER THE GREAT
Test, Page 2

2. What kind of people were plebeians?

   _____

   _____

3. Write a brief summary of the legend of the founding of Rome.

   _____

   _____

   _____

   _____

4. Name two books that Homer wrote.

   _____

   _____

5. In chronological order list all the events studied to date.

   Next to each write the appropriate date.

   _____

   _____

   _____

   _____

   _____

   _____

   _____

   _____

   _____

   _____

ARCHITECTURAL ADVANCES IN ROME
Worksheet

1. What is the approximate date of the architectural advances in Rome?

   _____

   _____

2. Where were the first Roman villages built?

   _____

   _____

3. When were the villages combined into one city?

   _____

   _____

4. When was the Roman forum built? What was it?

   _____

   _____

   _____

   _____

5. What were basilicas?

   _____

   _____

6. For what were Roman temples used?

   _____

   _____

   _____

   _____

7. When was a wall built to enclose the city of Rome?

   _____

   _____

ARCHITECTURAL ADVANCES IN ROME
Worksheet, Page 2

8. What was the purpose of the roads that were built in Rome?

_____

_____

_____

9. What were aqueducts?

_____

_____

_____

_____

_____

_____

_____

ARCHITECTURAL ADVANCES IN ROME
Project—Literature Unit
Detectives in Togas Study Guide

Detectives in Togas by Henry Winterfield

The book *Detectives in Togas* gives a practical understanding of how Roman life and government was practiced. This is a good time to begin reading the book.

CHAPTER ONE
1. What was written on the writing tablet hanging on the wall?
2. Why was Rufus mad at Caius?
3. Who was the father of Caius? Who was the father of Rufus?
4. What started the fight between Rufus and Caius?
5. What was the punishment for Caius? For Rufus?

CHAPTER TWO
1. Who was absent the next day of school?
2. What were three things the students thought could have happened to Xantippus?
3. Who was Lukos?
4. What is a soothsayer?
5. What was missing from the wall?

CHAPTER THREE
1. What were the only two items still upright in the room of Xantippus?
2. From where was the noise coming in the room?
3. What was making a moaning noise?
4. What had happened to Xantippus the night before?

CHAPTER FOUR
1. The burglar was rummaging through the things. What does rummaging mean?
2. Why did Xantippus not want to get the police involved?

3. What is a pupil?
4. Describe Minerva Square.
5. What was written on the whitewashed wall? What color was the paint?

CHAPTER FIVE
1. What did the large man think the punishment should have been for writing on the wall?
2. Who was Claudia?
3. What does it mean when the boys were wanting to exile Caius for telling on Rufus?
4. What did the boys plan to do with Rufus to hide him?
5. What did Rufus say about the writing on the temple wall?

CHAPTER SIX
1. Why did all the boys like Rufus so much?
2. What convinced Publius and Antonius that Rufus wrote on the wall?
3. What did the boys find under the wardrobe just as they were leaving?
4. Who did Xantippus say the chain belonged to?

CHAPTER SEVEN
1. What are hieroglyphs?
2. What was the large crowd standing around looking at when the boys came into the Forum?
3. What was so fascinating about the newspaper?

ARCHITECTURAL ADVANCES IN ROME
Project, Page 2—Literature Unit
Detectives in Togas Study Guide

CHAPTER EIGHT
1. Why did the doorkeeper tell the boys to enter with their right foot forward?
2. What was Vinicius doing when the boys entered the room?
3. Who is Scribonus?
4. What did Scribonus say about the handwriting on the wall and the handwriting on the tablet?

CHAPTER NINE
1. What had happened when the boys reached the house of Rufus?
2. What is a hoodlum?
3. What is the name of Rufus' mother?
4. Why would it have been impossible for Rufus to sneak out of the house in the middle of the night?
5. Why did Rompus come back so quickly?

CHAPTER TEN
1. What was the important news Rompus brought to Livia?
2. How did Rufus sneak out of his house?
3. What is the only thing the boys had to go by that linked the two crimes together?
4. Whose house were they going to go to seek advice?

CHAPTER ELEVEN
1. Describe the weather when the boys met in Minerva Square.
2. What did the boys see when they looked through the pane of yellow glass?
3. What was the reaction of Lukos when the boys asked him for help?
4. Who thought they had been bitten by a snake, but it was really only his dagger?
5. Who was missing from the group at the end of this chapter?

CHAPTER TWELVE
1. What had actually happened to Mucius?
2. What does the word ridiculous mean?
3. Why did Mucius want to get out of Lukos' house so badly?
4. What happened to Mucius when he fell off the roof?
5. What were the Baths of Diana?

Chapter Thirteen
1. What proof did the Arab have that Mucius had been in the Baths of Diana the night before?
2. What caused the superior in charge of the pool to change his bad attitude toward Mucius?
3. Why was it impossible for Rufus to be guilty of the writing on the temple?

CHAPTER FOURTEEN
1. Who's house is the only one around that is as high as the Baths?
2. Who was the one person that the boys needed to tell their story to?
3. What three things concerning the letter to the Emperor did the boys argue about?
4. Who finally admitted to writing on the temple wall?

CHAPTER FIFTEEN
1. Who showed up at the cave with the boys leaning on a stick?
2. On what did the boys write the letter to the Emperor?
3. What does Xantippus give as a definition for a hypothesis?
4. What did Xantippus say that made Rufus completely innocent?

ARCHITECTURAL ADVANCES IN ROME

Project, Page 3—Literature Unit
Detectives in Togas Study Guide

CHAPTER SIXTEEN
1. Who stood at the entrance to the Censor's office?
2. What was the name of the official who takes the late news at night?
3. Who brought Megabates the letter?

CHAPTER SEVENTEEN
1. Who was Ex-consul Tellus?
2. Write a one sentence summary of this chapter.

CHAPTER EIGHTEEN
1. About how long was Antonius gone on the important mission?
2. What two important items did Antonius return with from the house of Tellus?
3. Who did everyone think committed the crime now?
4. What is the meaning of, 'Tear the sheep's clothing off the red wolf?'

CHAPTER NINETEEN
1. What two things did Antonius recognize that convinced him it was Tellus walking in the Forum?
2. Who was inside the house of Lukos?
3. What happened when the boys went to spy on Lukos?
4. How does this chapter end?

CHAPTER TWENTY
1. Why was Lukos so bent on hurting Rufus?
2. Who hit Lukos over the back?
3. What are cothurns?
4. Who was the red wolf?
5. Who was Lukos really?

CHAPTER TWENTY-ONE
1. Who was the first one to find out about Lukos' dirty secret?
2. Why did Tellus not throw the chain away?
3. What was the agreement Tellus wanted to make with the boys?
4. Who is the one that rescued the boys?
5. What happened to Tellus?

CHAPTER TWENTY-TWO
1. What did the sign say that was added to the door of Lukos?
2. What was the mistake Xantippus admitted to making?
3. Summarize the ending of the book.
4. Was Xantippus being cruel when he said this?

ARCHITECTURAL ADVANCES IN ROME

Project, Page 4—Literature Unit
Detectives in Togas Study Guide

Answers

Chapter 1
1. Caius is a dumbell
2. He wouldn't let him study. He kept poking him in the back.
3. The wealthy senator Vinicius, famous general Marcus Praetonius
4. Caius called Rufus the son of a coward because his father had just lost an important battle.
5. Caius had to write every word in the list ten times in his best handwriting. Rufus was expelled from school.

Chapter 2
1. Caius and Rufus
2. Overslept, sick, or murdered
3. A famous astrologer and seer from Alexandria
4. Someone who knows what is going to happen in the future
5. The writing tablet

Chapter 3
1. The bed and a large wardrobe
2. The corner where the wardrobe stood
3. Xantippus was all tied up making the noise
4. He had been assaulted

Chapter 4
1. To go through without any pattern or organization
2. Because he did not think they were too smart, and they never found the burglar
3. A student
4. It was a quiet, open space surrounded by pine woods where wealthy mansions stood.
5. Caius is a dumbell; it was blood-red

Chapter 5
1. Cut both hands off
2. She was Caius' younger sister, and was well-liked by his classmates
3. They were not going to talk to him or play with him anymore.
4. They wanted to dress him like a slave and he would pretend to be one until the whole affair calmed down.
5. He said he did not do it.

Chapter 6
1. He was a good sport, and always full of fun and good ideas for games.
2. The handwriting was the exact same as Rufus'.
3. A short, wide gold chain
4. The burglar

Chapter 7
1. Egyptian picture writing
2. The daily newspaper
3. The article was about the writing on the temple wall.

Chapter 8
1. To ward off the misfortune it would bring upon the household if anyone entered with his left foot foremost.
2. He was getting a massage by two slaves.
3. The outstanding handwriting expert in Rome
4. They were written by the same person.

Chapter 9
1. He had been arrested.
2. Someone who commits petty crimes
3. Livia
4. Because the door was well locked and guarded, the windows were too small, and the garden was too high to climb.

5. To bring Livia some important news

Chapter 10
1. The master had won a great victory
2. Through a hole in the wall that had been covered up with ivy
3. The gold chain they had found
4. Lukos

Chapter 11
1. Foul; chilly with dirty-gray rain clouds
2. A frightful, grimacing face, illuminated by a greenish light, staring at them; it was only just a mask
3. He yelled at them to get out, and threw snakes at them.
4. Antonius
5. Mucius

Chapter 12
1. He had curiously stayed at Lukos' house.
2. Crazy, absurd
3. Because he was very scared of Lukos and what he might do to him.
4. He fell into an unknown river of water.
5. A place of recreation for rich patricians

Chapter 13
1. He had the lantern with Mucius' name on it that Rufus had accidentally taken.
2. Mucius mentioned who his father was.
3. Because he had been locked up at the Baths of Diana all night.

Chapter 14
1. Lukos
2. The Emperor
3. How it ought to be addressed, every sentence, and the signature
4. Caius

Chapter 15
1. Xantippus
2. A copy of Cicero's oration.
3. A statement which must be proved before it is accepted as true.
4. The newspaper article was printed before the writing even occurred.

Chapter 16
1. An armed guard
2. Megabates
3. Ex-consul Tellus

Chapter 17
1. He used to be a great general, and was a close friend of the Emperor.
2.

Chapter 18
1. Two hours
2. The chain, and the cloak of Tellus
3. Tellus
4.

Chapter 19
1. His bald head, and the scar.
2. Tellus
3. He locked them in his house.
4. Lukos says he was the desecrator of the temple.

Chapter 20
1. He had discovered his greatest secret and must die.
2. Caius
3. Shoes with high wooden soles, actors wear them on stage.
4. Lukos
5. Tellus

ARCHITECTURAL ADVANCES IN ROME
Project, Page 6—Literature Unit
Detectives in Togas Study Guide

Chapter 21
1. Rufus
2. It was a good luck token he was given
in the East.
3. If the boys keep the secret of Lukos,
then he will send a messenger to free
Rufus.
4. Xantippus
5. He jumped off the roof a little too late
and landed into the empty Baths.

Chapter 22 —The Final Chapter
1. Moved to Hades
2. He allowed himself to be carried away
by anger.
3. Xantippus laughed until tears rolled
down his cheeks and said, "Caius, you
really are a dumbell."
4. No, he said it endearingly.

ARCHITECTURAL ADVANCES IN ROME

Project, Page 7—Literature Unit
Detectives in Togas Study Guide

Map of the City

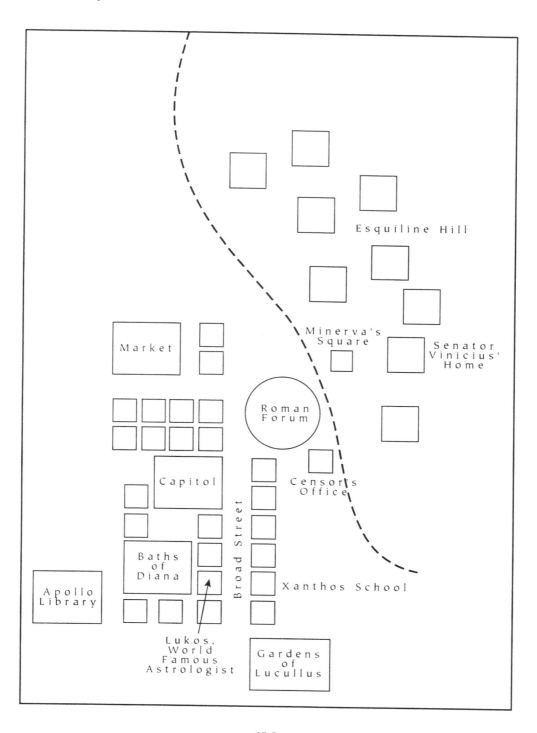

ARCHITECTURAL ADVANCES IN ROME
Project 2

Using pages 18 and 19 from *The Usborne Illustrated World History, The Romans* answer the following questions:

1. Why did the Romans develop their system of roads?

_____

_____

_____

_____

2. What was the first major road and when was it begun?

_____

_____

_____

_____

3. On the next page draw a picture to illustrate how the Romans built their roads.

   Using pages 30 and 31 of the same book answer the following:

4. Were the Roman towns set up with any particular plan or design?

_____

_____

_____

5. What was the forum?

_____

_____

6. On the next page draw a picture of a typical Roman town.

   Be sure to include the thermae, the forum, temples, the amphitheater and a basilica

ARCHITECTURAL ADVANCES IN ROME
Project 2, Page 2

How the Romans built their roads:

A typical Roman town:

ARCHITECTURAL ADVANCES IN ROME
Project 2, Page 3

7. Using pages 34, 35, 44-47, 60, or 61 choose one of the following to illustrate and label the different parts: a domus, an insulae, a Roman villa, an imperial farm or the baths.

8. What civilization greatly influenced Roman architecture?

_____

_____

9. Before the Romans, most buildings were constructed with walls and _____ topped by beams of _____ or _____ . The largest known _____ span built in this way is 25 feet. They developed an _____ which enabled builders to span greater distances.

ARCHITECTURAL ADVANCES IN ROME
Project 2, Page 4

10. What was a further development of the arch that was made by crossing a number of arches over each other to enclose a circular area?

_____

_____

_____

_____

11. Draw a picture of the Pantheon.

ARCHITECTURAL ADVANCES IN ROME
Test

1. What is the approximate date of Architectural advances in Rome?

_____

_____

2. What do seven hills have to do with the beginning of Rome?

_____

_____

3. Who combined the Roman villages into one city?

_____

_____

4. What was the Roman forum?

_____

_____

5. What were basilicas?

_____

_____

6. To whom were most of the temples dedicated?

_____

_____

7. As the population of Rome grew, how did they organize the city?

_____

_____

8. How did the Romans bring fresh water to the city?

_____

_____

9. What did the Romans develop to carry away dirty water?

_____

_____

Review

1. What is sophistry?

_____

_____

2. Who fought in the Persian wars in c. 500 B. C.?

_____

_____

3. Name two prophets of God?

_____

_____

4. How did the early Greeks explain the world around them?

_____

_____

5. List in chronological order all the events studied to date.

    Place the appropriate date next to each one.

_____

_____

_____

_____

_____

ROME RISES TO WORLD POWER
Worksheet

1. By what date had Rome risen to world power?

   _____

   _____

2. In the year 146 B.C. how did Corinth resist Rome?

   _____

   _____

   _____

3. In the third of the three "Punic Wars" who did Rome destroy?

   _____

   _____

4. Why was Rome now recognized as the capital of the world?

   _____

   _____

   _____

5. Why were the Romans considered to be in a "class by themselves?"

   _____

   _____

   _____

ROME RISES TO WORLD POWER
Project

Using *The Usborne Illustrated World History, The Romans* pages 8, 9, answer the following questions:

1. While Rome was becoming powerful in _____, the western Mediterranean was under the control of the _____.

2. Where was Carthage located? Who founded it?

_____

_____

_____

3. What was the cause of the Punic Wars? Who was involved in them?

_____

_____

_____

4. Why were they called the Punic Wars?

_____

_____

5. How many Punic wars were there in total?

_____

_____

_____

6. What happened as a result of the third Punic War?

_____

_____

_____

_____

ROME RISES TO WORLD POWER
Project, Page 2

7. What happened as a result of the Romans crushing Corinth In 146 B.C.?

_____

_____

Using *The Usborne Illustrated World History, The Romans* page 10, answer the following questions:

1. Who were the cives?

_____

_____

2. Who were the peregrini?

_____

_____

3. At first only people with _____ parents qualified for citizenship. Later the government began granting citizenship to certain _____. This caused further division of the classes.

4. Name the three classes of citizens and describe them.

_____

_____

_____

5. Who were the non-citizens?

_____

_____

6. Who was the head of a Roman family?

_____

_____

ROME RISES TO WORLD POWER
Project 2

Study the map below in order to review the following with your class:

1. Roman territory at the beginning of the Punic Wars

2. Land acquired as a result of the First Punic Wars

3. Land acquired as a result of the Second Punic Wars

4. Land acquired as a result of a Third Punic War

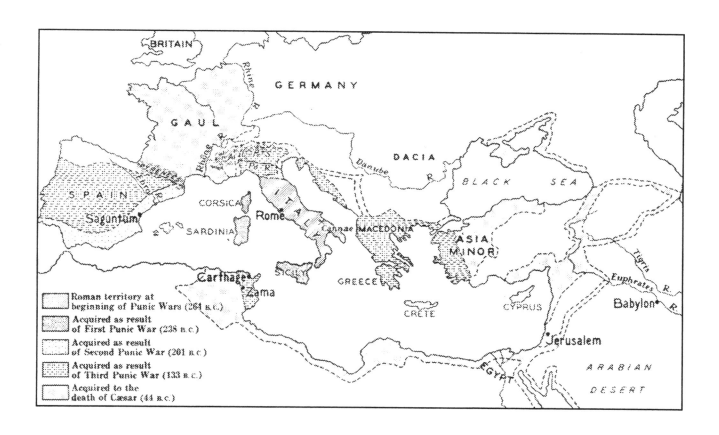

ROME RISES TO WORLD POWER
Project 3

The instructions for this project can be found on Appendix 2-1.

The Rise of Roman Power and the Decline of the Roman Republic

I

Rome did not become the major power in the Mediterranean World overnight. It was a long, slow process. The first step was to gain control of the Italian peninsula. They first had to gain their independence from the Etruscans and then fight difficult wars against the Samnites in the East and the Greeks in the South. After gaining control of Italy, Rome found itself almost immediately in conflict with Carthage, a great city in northern Africa that had originally been settled by the Phoenicians. They were to fight three wars with Carthage, which were known as the "Punic Wars", after the Latin word for "Phoenician." The Second Punic War saw the dramatic invasion by the Carthaginian general Hannibal over the Alps and into Italy. When the Roman general Scipio finally defeated Hannibal in the battle of Zama, Rome became the undisputed master of the Western Mediterranean.

II

The year 146 BC was a big year for Rome. It marked the end of the Third Punic war and the complete destruction of Carthage. It was also the year when Rome destroyed Corinth. Perseus, the last of the Hellenistic rulers of the "Antigonid" dynasty of Macedonia, had already been defeated in 168 BC at the battle of Pydna. Corinth, however, long a merchant capital and naval power, was the center of a renewed Greek revolt against Roman rule. Though it had long been considered one of the best fortified cities in Greece, Rome conquered it without too much difficulty and it met the same fate as Carthage. The largest of the Hellenistic kingdoms, the Seleucid kingdom of Asia posed little threat. They had been fighting among themselves so much that they didn't have much of an army for Rome to conquer. The last of the great Hellenistic kingdoms was the Ptolemaic kingdom of Egypt. Its last ruler was Cleopatra, who eventually allied herself with Mark Antony. When Octavian defeated Antony and Cleopatra at the battle of Actium, Egypt became a part of the Roman Empire. The end of Carthage and the Hellenistic kingdoms made gave Rome control over all of the Mediterranean.

III

Unfortunately, as Rome was increasing, the Republic was decreasing. As the wars that Rome fought grew ever larger and farther away, certain popular generals became more and more powerful and eventually even challenged the authority of the Roman Senate. Julius Caesar was a perfect example of just such a power-hungry general. When his nephew Octavian succeeded him, he is generally thought to have begun a new era in which there was now an emperor who was no longer accountable to the Senate or the people of Rome.

Vocabulary

1. *dramatic:* _____

   _____

2. *invasion:* _____

   _____

3. *undisputed:* _____

   _____

4. *Hellenistic:* _____

   _____

5. *peninsula:* _____

   _____

6. *fortified:* _____

   _____

7. *dynasty:* _____

   _____

Key Word Outline

I _____

  1 _____

  2 _____

  3 _____

  4 _____

  5 _____

  6 _____

ROME RISES TO WORLD POWER
Project 3, Page 3

7 _____

8 _____

II _____

1 _____

2 _____

3 _____

4 _____

5 _____

6 _____

7 _____

8 _____

9 _____

10 _____

11 _____

12 _____

III _____

1 _____

2 _____

3 _____

4 _____

ROME RISES TO WORLD POWER
Project 3, Page 4

Answers
Vocabulary
1. *dramatic:* involving great, violent conflict
2. *invasion:* large-scale attack
3. *undisputed:* not contested
4. *Hellenistic:* Greek in culture
5. *peninsula:* a stretch of land surrounded by water on three sides
6. *fortified:* built strong to resist attack
7. *dynasty:* a ruling family

Key Word Outline
I. Rome's Mastery of the West
1. Not, power, overnight
2. Slow, process
3. Gain, control, peninsula
4. Win, independence, fight
5. Conflict, Carthage
6. Three, Punic, Wars
7. Second, invasion, Hannibal
8. Scipio, defeated, Hannibal

II. Rome's Mastery of the Mediterranean
1. 146, big, year
2. Marked, end, Carthage
3. Rome, destroyed
4. Macedonia, defeated, Pydna
5. Corinth, center, revolt
6. Though, fortified, conquered
7. Seleucid, little, threat
8. Fighting, among, themselves
9. Last, Ptolemaic, Egypt
10. Cleopatra, allied, Mark Antony
11. Octavian, defeated, Actium
12. Rome, control, Mediterranean

III. The Decline of the Roman Republic
1. Republic, decreasing
2. Generals, more, powerful
3. Julius Caesar, example
4. Octavian, succeeded, emperor

ROME RISES TO WORLD POWER
Test

1. By what date had Rome risen to world power?

   _____

   _____

2. What is meant by the statement that Rome had risen to world power?

   _____

   _____

3. In 146 B. C. how was Corinth able to resist Rome?

   _____

   _____

4. Who did the Romans destroy in the third Punic War?

   _____

   _____

5. Why was Rome recognized as the capital of the world?

   _____

   _____

6. Why were Romans considered to be in a class by themselves?

   _____

   _____

Review

1. What was the title of the book written by Homer about the Trojan War?

   _____

   _____

   _____

ROME RISES TO WORLD POWER
Test, Page 2

2. What was the Phoenicians greatest contribution to civilization?

_____

_____

3. What was the first European civilization and where did it begin?

_____

_____

4. Two philosophical groups of people formed; the Stoics and Epicurians.
   Describe these two groups.

_____

_____

_____

5. List in chronological order all the events studied to date.
   Next to each place the appropriate date and Scripture reference where applicable.

_____

_____

_____

_____

_____

_____

_____

_____

_____

_____

REIGN OF JULIUS CAESAR
Worksheet

1. What are the dates for the Reign of Julius Caesar?

   _____

   _____

2. In to what kind of family was Julius Caesar born?

   _____

   _____

3. Approximately when was Julius Caesar born?

   _____

   _____

4. What disciplines did Julius Caesar study?

   _____

   _____

   _____

5. What land did Julius Caesar conquer in 58 B.C.?

   _____

   _____

6. How did Julius Caesar become Rome's ruler?

   _____

   _____

7. Name three things that Julius Caesar improved as Rome's ruler.

   _____

   _____

   _____

REIGN OF JULIUS CAESAR
Worksheet, Page 2

8. Why was he stabbed to death on March 15, 44 B.C.?

_____

_____

_____

9. Caesar's heir was _____(Caesar's friend), who joined Mark Antony

   to defeat the men who killed _____.

   These two men ruled the Empire for _____ years.

REIGN OF JULIUS CAESAR
Project

Life of Caesar

Caesar in Gaul

When Julius Caesar was a young man, he was taken by pirates. He sent his servants to collect money for his ransom, and then set out to make merry with his captors. When he was tired, he told them to keep quiet and let him sleep. When he wanted to be amused, he told them to dance and entertain him, and the strange part of it is that they obeyed. He composed verses, and he rated them for their stupidity. "You don't know poetry when you hear it," he said. "You think you can scoff at my verses and orations because I am a prisoner. I'll take you prisoner some day, and then you shall have your pay." "What will it be?" they demanded with shouts of laughter. "I'll crucify every one of you," he replied quietly. Not so long after this he kept his word; but the Romans laughed at him for being so tenderhearted as to have their throats cut before they were crucified.

A few years later, Caesar was made governor of Spain. As a general thing, when a man becomes governor of a providence, his chief aim was to get as much money from the provincials as possible, but Caesar behaved as if he were really interested in his people and wanted to help them. He completed the conquest of Spain, and he straightened out the financial affairs of the province. Then he returned to Rome. The people's party made him consul, but the nobles succeeded in electing one of their own party to be second consul. Caesar was so much stronger than he that the jokers of the time used to date their papers, "In the courtship of Julius and Caesar."

There were now in Rome three men of power; Crassus, who was enormously rich; Pompey, who had long been a successful general; and Caesar, who had not yet accomplished so very much, but who had the power to make people believe that he could do whatever he chose to undertake. These three men, the First Triumvirate, as they are called, bargained together to help one another and divide the Roman world among them.

Caesar's share in this division was Gaul, the present day France, and he set off to conquer the country. Before long, wonderful stories came back to Rome of great victories and the capture of thousands of prisoners. Trees were cut down in the forest, and in a few days they had been made into complicated bridges. Great chiefs yielded and cities surrendered. There were tales of forced marches, of sudden surprises, of vast amounts of booty, also of a mysterious land across the water to the northwest. It was called Britain, and tin was brought from there, but no one knew much about it, not even whether it was an island or not. By and by, Caesar visited this Britain. He wrote a book about the country

REIGN OF JULIUS CAESAR
Project, Page 2

and his conquests there and about his campaigns in Gaul. It is called his "Commentaries," and is so clear and simple and concise that it is a model of military description. The Triumvirate had agreed that Pompey should give up his command in Spain and Caesar in Gaul at the same time; but Pompey remained near Rome, and he induced the Senate to allow him to continue as governor of Spain for five years longer. Then Caesar was aroused. At the end of the five years, he would be only a private citizen, while Pompey would be

commander of a great army. Crassus was dead. "Either decree that Pompey and I shall give up our provinces at the same time, or allow me to stand for the consulship before I enter Rome," Caesar urged. The Senate refused and moreover threatened two magistrates, called tribunes of the people, who stood by Caesar. They fled to his camp on the farther side of the little river Rubicon.

It was a law in Rome that any Roman general who brought his army across the Rubicon should be regarded as an enemy to his country. Caesar could declare now, however, that he was coming, not as an enemy, but to defend the people and and their tribunes against Pompey and the nobles. It is said that he hesitated, then exclaimed, "The die is cast," and plunged into the river, followed by his army.

Pompey fled. Caesar made himself master of Italy and then pursued Pompey. At Pharsalus in Thessaly a great battle was fought, and Caesar won. Pompey fled to Egypt for protection, but the Egyptian councilors were afraid of Caesar and killed the fugitive. Caesar returned to Rome the ruler of the world. He had a magnificent triumph, and he gave the people feasts and money and combats of wild beasts, their favorite amusement. The senators were thoroughly humbled. They made him dictator for life; they changed the name of his birth-month from Quintilis (fifth) to Julius (July); they stamped their money with his image; they even dedicated temples and altars to him as to a god. Caesar's head was not turned by this flattery, but the heads of those who had opposed him were almost turned with astonishment and relief. Some years before this, one general named Marius and then another one named Sulla had held sole rule in Rome, and each of them had put to death some thousand of people who had been against him. The Romans supposed that

REIGN OF JULIUS CAESAR
Project, Page 3

Caesar would behave in the same way, but he made no attempt to revenge himself. Indeed, his only thought seemed to be to do what was best for Rome. He made just laws for rich and poor, and was especially thoughtful of the good of the provincials. He planned to collect a great library, to put up magnificent temples and other public buildings, to rebuild Carthage, to make a road along the Apennines, and to drain the Pontine Marshes, which were near the city. Caesar ruled nobly, but a plot was formed against him. The chief conspirators were Cassius and Brutus. Cassius was envious of his great power, Brutus believed that if Caesar were slain, the old forms of government would be restored and Rome would be again a republic. These men pressed about Caesar in the senate house as if they wished to present him a petition. At a signal, they drew their swords. Caesar defended himself for a moment; then he saw among them the face of Brutus, the one to whom he had shown every favor and to whom he had given a sincere affection. He cried, "You, too, Brutus!", drew his robe over his face, and fell dead. It was the custom for an oration to be delivered at a funeral. The conspirators very unwisely permitted Caesar's friend Antony to speak at his funeral. He also read Caesar's will, in which he had left a gift of money to every citizen and had been especially generous to some of the very men who had become his murderers. The people were aroused to such a pitch of fury that the assassins were glad to flee from the city. The senate appointed Antony to see that the will was carried out, and they agreed to accept as ruler a grandnephew of Caesar whom he had named as his successor. This grandnephew was a young man named Octavianus, who afterwards became the emperor Augustus.

After reading the above information on Julius Caesar fill in the circles on the following page, with what you believe to be the most important events in Caesar's life. Illustrate each one and provide a caption.

REIGN OF JULIUS CAESAR
Test

1. What are the dates that Julius Caesar reigned?

   _____

   _____

2. In approximately what year was Julius Caesar born?

   Into what kind of family was he born?

   _____

   _____

   _____

3. List the disciplines that Julius Caesar studied over his educational years.

   _____

   _____

   _____

4. How did Caesar become ruler of Rome?

   _____

   _____

5. List at least three improvements that Caesar made as Rome's ruler.

   _____

   _____

   _____

6. Did all the Roman's love Julius Caesar?

   _____

   _____

   _____

REIGN OF JULIUS CAESAR
Test

7. How did Caesar die?

_____

_____

_____

8. Who became ruler at Caesar's death?

_____

_____

_____

Review

1. What was Nehemiah's occupation?

_____

_____

2. Who won the Peleponnesian War?

_____

_____

3. Why did God become angry at Solomon and divide his kingdom?

_____

_____

4. Where does democracy find its roots?

_____

_____

5. On the back list in chronological order all the events studied to date.

   Next to each place the appropriate dates and Biblical reference.

REIGN OF CAESAR AUGUSTUS
Worksheet

1. Octavian and Mark Antony had been ruling the Roman Empire together.
   Which one rose up against the other to gain control of the Empire?

   _____

   _____

2. Who became the sole ruler of Rome in 30 A.D.? To what did he change his name?

   _____

   _____

3. What was the "Pax Romana"?

   _____

   _____

4. During the reign of Caesar Augustus, the government changed from a _____

   to a _____.

5. Caesar established 30 to 40 officials under him to help make a better government.
   What were some of these positions?

   _____

   _____

6. For how long did Augustus rule?

   _____

   _____

7. Why did the Romans accept this one man rule?

   _____

   _____

8. Who was Emperor when Christ was born?

   _____

   _____

REIGN OF CAESAR AUGUSTUS
Project

The Reign of Caesar Augustus

CAIUS JULIUS CAESAR OCTAVIANUS was an exceedingly wise young man. He had seen his uncle lose his life, not because he did not govern well, but because the Romans suspected that he meant to take the title of king. This new ruler believed that it was far more desirable to have power than to have any special title. Moreover, he had learned that a large number of citizens were startled at any suggestion of new laws or abrupt changes, but were contented if the old names and forms of government were kept up. Therefore he called himself simply imperator, a military title meaning hardly more than commander. He never spoke of his victory over Antonius as the triumph of any party, but merely as the successful ending of an Eastern war. He was made consul and he voted in the senate just as any consul might do. He wore no royal robes, but the ordinary dress of a Roman. His house was like the dwellings of other men of good position, but not pretentious in any way. The people believed that the government was moving on in the old fashion, the senators held their regular meetings and felt that they were deciding all important matters; and yet, little by little, the control of every division of the government was coming into the hands of Octavianus.

Apparently, he held his power with a loose grasp. Sometimes he would offer to give up some of it. Surely, there was no reason to be jealous of a ruler who seemed to have no ambition but to do his best to govern well; and so he came to be at the head of one branch of the government after another. He became censor; *princeps,* or first senator and pontifex maximus, or chief priest. Finally, he was given the title of *Augustus,* or the *Majestic, the Revered,* and it is by this title that he is usually spoken of in history. Sextilis, the name of the month in which his first consulate began, was changed to August in his honor.

By this quiet way of controlling the state, the clear-headed imperator, or emperor, was able to bring about what he wanted. One thing that both he and his people wanted was peace. He was obliged to carry on warfare to some extent during his reign, but he did not attempt to make the empire larger. He believed rather that Rome had as wide a dominion as she could well govern, but that it ought to be bounded by mountains, rivers, deserts, or seas, that is, by natural boundaries. As far as possible, he carried out this scheme. He would have liked to take the Elbe for part of the northern boundary; but the German tribes south of that river rebelled, and the Roman army under Varus was utterly destroyed. This almost broke the emperor's heart. It is said that he used to cry out in agony even in his dreams, "O Varus, Varus, give me back my legions!" The Rhine and the Danube became the northern limits of the empire. If a line be drawn from the mouth of the Rhine to Cape St. Vincent in Portugal, and that line be moved on to the southeast until it has gone beyond Syria and Egypt, the boundaries so marked will include little that was not under Roman rule.

To make the most of what Rome already held was Augustus' aim. A glance at the story of the dishonest governor, Verres, shows how badly the provinces needed attention and help. Augustus gave these generously. The newer and less peaceful provinces he kept in his own bands. He appointed a governor for each, paid him a salary, and forbade the oppression of the natives. If a governor disobeyed, he was punished. The other provinces

REIGN OF CAESAR AUGUSTUS
Project, Page 2

were left in the hands of the senate, but they were not forgotten, for Augustus kept close watch of their governors and saw that the provincials were fairly treated. He was always ready to listen to any complaint from them. After the Social War, a man in Italy or in the provinces who had been made a Roman citizen, had a right to vote, but in reality he was ruled by the people who lived in Rome, as has been said before, because they alone could conveniently be present at the assemblies. Now that Augustus had become the one power in Rome, it was gradually coming about that the citizens in Rome had no more power than those hundreds of miles away, for the emperor ruled them all.

The Romans thought it an important part of a ruler's duty to amuse them, and this duty Augustus never neglected. Unfortunately, their favorite amusement was the gladiatorial contest. The emperor made most liberal arrangements for this. He provided wild beasts by the hundred and gladiators by the thousand. "Bread and the games of the circus!" was the cry of the people of Rome, and the state supplied both. The laws of Caius Gracchus, passed more than a century earlier, allowed every Roman citizen to buy grain of the state at half price or less. The privilege had been continued, and the number who depended upon this charity had increased until in the time of Augustus it is probable that fully half of Rome received their food or part of it from the government. Of course some of these people were not able to earn their support; but the others deliberately preferred to ask bread of the state rather than earn it. There was the same old desire of the poor to avoid work; and with it went the eagerness of the rich to find new luxuries.

Augustus was interested in architecture, and he put up many temples, for men were forgetting their old reverence for the gods, and he wished to do all that he could to restore it. Anyone walking through the city would see handsome buildings, such as the Capitol, the Pantheon, or temple of all the gods, the senate house, and *basilica* or hall of justice. There were now several handsome forums in the city, and these public squares, as well as the temples, were adorned with statues. There were beautiful parks and public gardens, and along the Campus Martius were porticoes, whose roofs were upheld by columns, and here people might walk in the shade. On the Palatine Hill were the luxurious homes of the wealthy, but the city as a whole must have been a vast collection of little houses and shops, with lanes, rather than streets, winding in and out among them.

The homes of the wealthy were most splendid. Even those that were in town were so surrounded by gardens and trees and vineyards that one within them might fancy himself many miles away from a city. The houses were full of luxury and gorgeousness, even though they were not always in the best of taste. The vestibule was often adorned with busts and statues, perhaps brought from some conquered city. The walls were painted with some bright color and frescoed. There were tables veneered with plates of gold, silver, or ivory, chairs of cedar, floors of marble or of mosaic work, couches on which to recline at meals, sometimes of bronze, and sometimes of wood inlaid with ivory or gold. The beds had silver legs, mattresses stuffed with down, silken pillows, and richly embroidered purple coverlets. There were beautiful ornaments, vases, and exquisite work in glass. There were most graceful lamps of terra cotta, bronze, or gold.

At their meals the Romans loaded the table as nations do that have more money than good taste, and a slave who could cook perfectly was worth one thousand times as much as an ordinary slave. Vegetables, eggs, fish, fowls of many sorts, peacocks, and wild boars roasted whole, pastries and fruits were used, but the Roman idea of a luxurious meal was one at which many strange dishes appeared. The farther these were brought and the rarer they were, the more delicious they were supposed to be. A dinner of six or seven elaborate courses followed by much drinking of wine was not thought to be a sufficient entertainment for guests, and they were amused by rope-dancers, conjurers, and singers.

To learn Greek was so much the fashion that a Greek slave was usually chosen to attend boy's a school that he might talk with them in his own language. They learned chiefly reading, writing, and arithmetic. In the reading class, the boys repeated together after the teacher, first the letters, then the syllables of a word, and finally the whole word. The books were of parchment folded into leaves or scrolls of Papyrus. The text had been copied on them by slaves. When it was time for the writing lesson, the boys took their tablets covered with wax and followed with a sharp point, or *stilus,* the letters that the teacher had traced. When they could do this well, they were allowed to make letters on the wax for themselves; and when they could write fairly well, they were promoted to use pens made of reeds, ink, and paper made from papyrus. Arithmetic they learned from an abacus, on whose wires little balls were strung. When the boys grew older, they attended more advanced schools, and in these the masterpieces of Greek literature were taught. Then many of them went on further and studied oratory. They were required to have Greek teachers, and those who could afford the expense went to Greece to complete their education.

The emperor was interested in literature, and the greatest of all the Latin writers lived during his reign. They were Virgil, Horace, Livy, and Ovid. Virgil, or Publius Virgilius Maro, wrote a long poem, the Æneid, or story of Eneas and his coming to Italy after the fall of Troy. The Romans had been so well pleased with his shorter poems that when they heard of his plan to write the, Æneid, they were delighted. They had a long time to wait before seeing the book, for Virgil was not at all strong, and it was seven years before it was half done. Then the emperor asked him to read what he had written. He read first about the night when the Greeks slid softly down from the wooden horse and Troy was taken and burned; then he read about Aeneas' stay in Carthage; and last, about his visit to the land of the dead. Here, the poem says, was the young Marcellus, whom the fates would "only show to the earth" and then snatch away. *"Fling lilies with o'erflowing hands, and let / Me strew his grave with violets,"* Virgil repeated. Marcellus was the name of a favorite nephew whom the emperor had adopted to be his successor. The young man had died only a little while before this, and the emperor was grateful that his name had been made immortal by the poet. In his will, Virgil directed the Æneid to be burned because he had not yet made it as perfect as he wished, but Augustus forbade that such a thing should be done. He gave the manuscript to three friends of Virgil, all of them poets, telling them to strike out any phrase that they thought Virgil would have omitted on revision, but to add nothing. So it was that the Æneid was saved.

Horace, or Quintus Horatius Flaccus, had studied in Greece, according to the fashion, and when a young man, had fought in the army of Brutus. Virgil introduced him to Mæcenas, a wealthy statesman who knew how to be a warm friend. Through Mæcenas he met the emperor, and here he was sure to find appreciation. He wrote no lengthy poem, but many short ones, graceful odes to Mæcenas, to Virgil, to the emperor, to the state, to a beautiful fountain. He understood so well how people feel that one might almost fancy his poems were written yesterday. He thoroughly likes a jest or an unexpected turn. In one poem, a usurer, or money-lender, tells how he longs to live in the country. "Happy is the man," he says, "who dwells on his own farm, far away from the troubles of the city. He can train his vines, or graft his trees, or shear his sheep, or lie on the soft grass and hear the birds sing and the little streams murmur." Then Horace ends, "So said the moneylender. He called in all his money on the fifteenth of the month to buy a home in the country but he forgot the country and loaned it again on the first of the following month." When Mæcenas was dying, he said to Augustus," Take care of Horace as if he were myself," but Horace lived only a few months longer than his good friend.

Livy, or Titus Livius, liked to think and talk of the days before the aristocratic notions of the Romans were overthrown by Caesar, and Augustus playfully called him a follower of

Pompey. Livy's great work was a history of the Roman people; and in his preface he says that it will be reward enough for his labor in writing it if he can only forget for a while the troubles of his own times. This sounds rather mournful, but the history is charming. In reading it we almost feel that we are listening to Livy himself, for he writes his stories of the olden times as if he were telling them to a group of friends. He describes something that pleases him as if he were sure that his readers would enjoy it with him, and he is as grieved over a lost battle of a century earlier as if the defeated general were his own dear friend.

Even when Ovid, or Publius Ovidius Naso, was a small boy he was eager to write poetry. His father wished him to become an orator and win some high position in the government, and the boy tried his best to learn to argue. His teacher said that he spoke in a poetical sort of prose and did not arrange his arguments well. After a while a fortune was left to him, and then he was free to write as much poetry as he chose. He was liked by the emperor, and life moved on most pleasantly. He wrote the *Metamorphoses,* or stories of the gods. One is the tale of the visit of Jupiter and Mercury to Baucis and Philemon. It is so simply and naturally told that we can almost see old Baucis building a fire on the hearth, putting a piece of a broken dish under one leg of the table so it will stand even, then rubbing the board with mint to make it smell sweet. Ovid was revising his manuscript one evening when an order for his banishment to the mouth of the Danube suddenly arrived from the emperor. No one ever knew why this was done. Ovid was torn from his family and sent to spend the rest of his life among the barbarians. In his despair he burned *the Metamorphoses* but fortunately his friends had made copies of it long before. He died in exile.

It is because these great writers lived in the times of Augustus that his reign is called the Golden, or Augustan, Age of Latin literature. The reign is also marked by the closing of the gates of the temple of Janus. In war times these were always open, and the Romans had carried on wars so constantly that the gates had been closed only twice in seven hundred years. While Augustus ruled, they were closed three times. It was during one of these times when the world was at peace that Jesus was born in Bethlehem.

REIGN OF CAESAR AUGUSTUS
Project 2

Making a Roman Theater Mask

Have children read pages 56 and 57 in *The Usborne Illustrated World History The Romans,* before making the mask.

Materials:
Paper plate for each child
    (inexpensive paper plate)
yarn
acrylic paint
    (variety of colors)
wallpaper paste
newspaper
large popsicle sticks
hot glue gun

Instructions
Step 1: Tear sheets of newspaper into strips about 1 inch wide. Tear these strips into small rectangular pieces of paper.
Step 2: Tape paper plate and cut out eyes, nose and mouth.
Step 3: Attach a cardboard piece using the cut out for the mouth to make a raised nose.
Step 4: Mix wallpaper paste and place newspaper into it. Let it absorb the paste.
Step 5: Apply layers of newspaper to mask building up layers, allowing to dry.
Step 6: Place yarn in wallpaper paste and apply to mask for hair, swirls work well. Allow to dry.
Step 7: When dry, paint with acrylic paint.
Step 8: Hot glue the popsicle stick to the back of the mask in order to be able to hold the mask up to face.

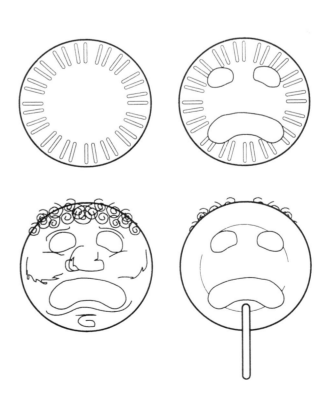

REIGN OF CAESAR AUGUSTUS
Project 3

Roman Writing Kit

When it was time for writing lessons, the boys took their tablets covered with wax and followed with a sharp point, or *stilus,* the letters that the teacher had traced. When they could do this well, they were allowed to make letters on the wax for themselves.

Supplies

disposable cake pans
   (purchasable at grocery store, 9" x 12")

old candles or wax

double boiler

shiskebab sticks

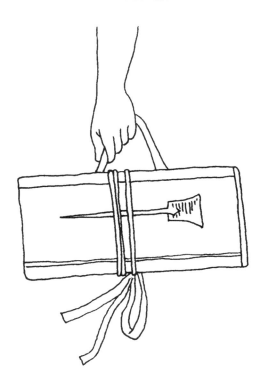

Directions
1. Melt wax or old candles in a double boiler over water. (If using candles it is best to break into pieces.)
2. After wax has melted pour into the cake pans. Allow to cool.
3. Use the stick to write on your tablet.

REIGN OF CAESAR AUGUSTUS
Test

1. Who became emperor of Rome in 30 A.D.? How did he become the ruler?

   _____

   _____

   _____

2. What was the time of peace in Rome called?

   _____

   _____

3. During the reign of Caesar Augustus, the government changed from a _____

   to a _____.

4. What did Caesar do in order to help establish a better government?
   List some of these jobs.

   _____

   _____

   _____

   _____

5. How many years did Caesar Augustus rule?

   _____

   _____

6. Why did the Roman people accept his one-man rule?

   _____

   _____

7. Who was the Roman Emperor when Christ was born?

   _____

   _____

REIGN OF CAESAR AUGUSTUS
Test, Page 2

Review

1. Who was Isaiah?

_____

_____

2. What reason does Scripture give that Israel and Judah fell?

_____

_____

3. By whom was Rome founded?

_____

_____

4. Describe the first Olympics.

_____

_____

_____

5. List in chronological order all the events studied to date.

   Next to each place the appropriate date and Scripture reference.

_____

_____

_____

_____

_____

_____

_____

BIRTH OF CHRIST
Worksheet

1. What is the approximate date for the birth of Christ?

   _____

   _____

2. What are the Scripture references for the birth of Christ?

   _____

   _____

3. Who came to tell Mary that she would be the mother of Jesus?

   _____

   _____

4. Why was Mary so surprised by the news
   that she would have a child?

   _____

   _____

5. To whom was Mary engaged?

   _____

   _____

6. Why when Mary was so close to giving birth,
   did she leave home and depart to Bethlehem?

   _____

   _____

   _____

   _____

BIRTH OF CHRIST
Worksheet, Page 2

7. Where was Jesus born?

   _____

   _____

8. How did the shepherds find out about the birth of Jesus?

   _____

   _____

   _____

9. What did the shepherds do when they heard about Christ's birth?

   _____

   _____

   _____

   _____

   _____

BIRTH OF CHRIST
Project

Newspaper Article

Pretend that you are a reporter, interviewing one of the shepherds who went to see the baby Jesus. On the next page write an article that will appear in the Jerusalem Gazette.

JERUSALEM GAZETTE

BIRTH OF CHRIST
Test

1. What is the approximate date of the birth of Christ?

   _____

   _____

2. What is the Scripture reference for the birth of Christ?

   _____

   _____

3. Who did the angel Gabriel appear to and tell her that she would be the mother of Jesus? Why was this so miraculous?

   _____

   _____

   _____

4. Who decreeded that a census should be taken around the birth of Christ? How did this affect the birth of Christ?

   _____

   _____

   _____

5. Describe where Christ was born.

   _____

   _____

   _____

6. How did the sheperds know about the birth of Christ?

   _____

   _____

   _____

   _____

7. Once the shepherds found out that the Christ child was born what did they do?

_____

_____

Review

1. Why was Rome recognized as the capital of the world by 146 B.C.?

_____

_____

2. What was the Phoenician's most important contribution to civilization?

_____

_____

3. The prophet Ahijah appeared to Jeroboam a servant of Solomon. He told him that God would give him _____ tribes of Israel to rule. (Fill in the correct number of tribes.)

4. Why did the Mycenean culture end?

_____

_____

5. In chronological order list all the events studied to date.

   Next to each place the appropriate date and Scripture reference if applicable.

_____

_____

_____

_____

_____

_____

MINISTRY OF JOHN THE BAPTIST
Worksheet

1. What are the Scripture references for the Ministry of John the Baptist?

   _____

   _____

2. What is the approximate date for the ministry of John the Baptist?

   _____

   _____

3. Who was the last Old Testament prophet?

   _____

   _____

4. Why was this last Old Testament prophet sent by God?

   _____

   _____

5. How and where did this last Old Testament prophet live?

   _____

   _____

6. Who baptized Jesus? What did he think about baptizing Jesus?

   _____

   _____

7. After Jesus was baptized what did God do?

   _____

   _____

8. After Jesus ministry began, _____,

   having served his God ordained purposes,

   _____ into the background.

MINISTRY OF JOHN THE BAPTIST
Project

Read Matthew 3, Mark 1, Luke 3, and John 1. Using complete sentences, write a paragraph describing the Biblical meaning in the picture below.

_____

_____

_____

_____

_____

_____

_____

_____

_____

_____

MINISTRY OF JOHN THE BAPTIST
Test

1. What is the approximate date of the Ministry of John the Baptist?

   _____

   _____

2. What are the Scripture references for John the Baptist?

   _____

   _____

3. John the Baptist was the last Old Testament _____.

4. What did God send John the Baptist to do?

   _____

   _____

5. Where and how did John the Baptist live?

   _____

   _____

6. What did John say when he saw Jesus coming to be baptized?

   _____

   _____

   _____

7. What happened after John baptized Jesus?

   _____

   _____

8. After Jesus's ministry began what happened to John the Baptist? Why?

   _____

   _____

   _____

   _____

MINISTRY OF JOHN THE BAPTIST
Test, Page 2

Review

1. Write a paragraph describing the legend of the founding of Rome.

_____

_____

_____

_____

_____

_____

_____

_____

2. Write a paragraph describing the Trojan War.

_____

_____

_____

_____

_____

_____

_____

_____

3. On the back, list in chronological order all the events studied to date.

   Write the approximate dates next to each.

MINISTRY OF CHRIST
Worksheet

1. What are the dates for the Ministry of Christ?

   _____

   _____

2. What three things marked Jesus' ministry on earth?

   _____

   _____

   _____

   _____

3. Why did many people follow Christ?

   _____

   _____

   _____

4. What was known about Christ's teaching?

   _____

   _____

   _____

5. What did many of the Jews think of Christ?

   _____

   _____

   _____

   _____

   _____

   _____

   _____

MINISTRY OF CHRIST
Project, Page 2

Below are three pictures depicting Jesus teaching and two different parables. Before working on the page discuss the meaning and purpose of parables. Then write out an answer to the question "What is a Parable?" in your own words on the lines provided. Then read the Scripture reference and write the meaning of each of the depicted parables in the boxes below the picture

What is a Parable?

_____

_____

_____

Laborers in the Vineyard
Matthew 20:1-16

The Rich Man and Lazarus
Luke 16:19-31

The Good Samaritan
Luke 10:30-37

MINISTRY OF CHRIST
Test

1. What are the dates for the ministry of Christ?

   _____

   _____

2. What three things marked Jesus' ministry on earth?

   _____

   _____

   _____

   _____

3. Many people followed Christ to hear Him _____ or receive a

   miraculous _____.

4. What was said of His teaching?

   _____

   _____

5. Why did many Jews not accept Christ as the Messiah?

   _____

   _____

Review

1. What was "Linear A?"

   _____

   _____

2. Describe Mycenaen culture.

   _____

   _____

   _____

MINISTRY OF CHRIST
Test, Page 2

3. What caused the God to divide Israel into two kingdoms?

_____

_____

4. Who was Homer?

_____

_____

5. In chronological order list all the events studied to date.
   Next to each place the approximate date.

_____

_____

_____

_____

_____

_____

_____

_____

_____

_____

_____

_____

_____

_____

_____

_____

CRUCIFIXION, RESURRECTION, AND ASCENSION OF CHRIST
Worksheet

1. What is the date for the Crucifixion, Resurrection and Ascension of Christ?

   _____

   _____

2. What are the Scripture references for the Crucifixion, Resurrection, and Ascension of Christ?

   _____

   _____

3. How did Jesus come into Jerusalem?

   _____

   _____

4. What is "Passion Week?"

   _____

   _____

5. Why did the chief priest and scribes seek to have Jesus put to death?

   _____

   _____

6. Who was Judas Iscariot?

   _____

   _____

7. How was Christ put to death? What did this fulfill?

   _____

   _____

   _____

CRUCIFIXION, RESURRECTION, AND ASCENSION OF CHRIST
Worksheet, Page 2

8. What happened three days after Christ death?

   _____

   _____

9. How many days after Christ resurrection, did he ascend into heaven to be seated
   with His Father?

   _____

   _____

10. Christ reigns in Heaven, having been given _____over all things by God
    the Father.

CRUCIFIXION, RESURRECTION, AND ASCENSION OF CHRIST
Project

Chronology of Passion Week

Below you will find six pictures of the last days of Christ. Identify each and number them so they are in order chronologically. Use your Bible and history card as references.

\# _____

_____

\# _____

_____

\# _____

_____

\# _____

_____

\# _____

_____

\# _____

_____

CRUCIFIXION, RESURRECTION, AND ASCENSION OF CHRIST
Test

1. Approximately when did the crucifixion, resurrection and ascension of Christ take place?

   _____

   _____

2. How did Jesus come into Jerusalem? What did many do when they saw him?

   _____

   _____

   _____

3. What is "Passion Week?"

   _____

   _____

4. Why did the chief priests and scribes want Jesus put to death?

   _____

   _____

5. Who was Judas Iscariot? What was he convinced to do?

   _____

   _____

   _____

6. What was fulfilled that was foretold by the prophet Isaiah?

   _____

   _____

7. What happened three days after Christ's death?

   _____

   _____

CRUCIFIXION, RESURRECTION, AND ASCENSION OF CHRIST
Test, Page 2

8. To whom did Christ appear after his death?

_____

_____

9. Over what did Christ triumph with His death and resurrection?

_____

_____

10. What happened to Christ forty days after his death?

_____

_____

Review

1. The Romans had two classes the plebeians and the patricians. Explain each.

_____

_____

2. Name two prophets of God.

_____

_____

3. Where did democracy begin?

_____

_____

4. Who were the Etruscans?

_____

_____

5. In chronological order list all the events studied to date on the back.

ROME BURNS, NERO PERSECUTES CHRISTIANS
Worksheet

1. In what year did the first full scale persecutions of Christian's begin?
   What also occurred in this year?

   _____

   _____

2. How old was Nero when he began to rule Rome?

   _____

   _____

3. When Nero came to rule he no longer allowed Christians to worship God.
   Why did he do this?

   _____

   _____

   _____

4. Who was blamed for the fires in Rome?

   _____

   _____

5. What did Nero do to the Christians?

   _____

   _____

6. What two apostles were possibly
   executed during this time?

   _____

   _____

7. What eventually happened to Nero?

   _____

   _____

ROME BURNS, NERO PERSECUTES CHRISTIANS
Project

Reading on Martyrdom

Throughout all of history there have been those martyred for the sake of Christ. After reading the paragraphs below, read what Scripture has to say about the persecution of Christians. Acts 7, I Corinthians 4:12, II Corinthians 4, Hebrews 13. After reading this discuss what it means to be persecuted for the sake of Christ.

THE FIRST PERSECUTION, UNDER NERO, A.D. 67

The first persecution of the Church took place in the year 67, under Nero, the sixth emperor of Rome. This monarch reigned for the space of five years, with tolerable credit to himself, but then gave way to the greatest extravagancy of temper, and to the most atrocious barbarities. Among other diabolical whims, he ordered that the city of Rome should be set on fire, which order was executed by his officers, guards, and servants. While the imperial city was in flames, he went up to the tower of Macaenas, played upon his harp, sung the song of the burning of Troy, and openly declared that 'he wished the ruin of all things before his death.' Besides the noble pile, called the Circus, many other palaces and houses were consumed; several thousands perished in the flames, were smothered in the smoke, or buried beneath the ruin.

This dreadful conflagration continued nine days; when Nero, finding that his conduct was greatly blamed, and a severe odium cast upon him, determined to lay the whole upon the Christians, at once to excuse himself, and have an opportunity of glutting his sight with new cruelties. This was the occasion of the first persecution; and the barbarities exercised on the Christians were such as even excited the commiseration of the Romans themselves. Nero even refined upon cruelty, and contrived all manner of punishments for the Christians that the most infernal imagination could design. In particular, he had some sewed up in skins of wild beasts, and then worried by dogs until they expired; and others dressed in shirts made stiff with wax, fixed to axletrees, and set on fire in his gardens, in order to illuminate them. This persecution was general throughout the whole Roman Empire; but it rather increased than diminished the spirit of Christianity. In the course of it, St. Paul and St. Peter were martyred.

To their names may be added, Erastus, chamberlain of Corinth; Aristarchus, the Macedonian, and Trophimus, and Ephesians, converted by St. Paul, and fellow-laborer with him, Joseph, commonly called Barabus, and Ananias, bishop of Damascus; each of the Seventy."

—*John Fox's Book of Martyrs*

Rome Burns, Nero Persecutes Christians
Project, Page 2

Therefore to stop the rumor [that Nero set fire to Rome], he falsely charged with guilt, and punished with the most fearful tortures, the persons commonly called Christians, who were hated for their enormities. Christus, the founder of that name, was put to death as a criminal by Pontius Pilate, procurator of Judea, in the reign of Tiberius, but the pernicious superstition, repressed for a time, broke out yet again, not only through Judea, where the mischief originated, but through the city of Rome also, whither all things horrible and discraceful flow, as to a common receptacle. Accordingly, first those were arrested who confessed they were Christians; next, on their information, a multitude were convicted, not so much on the charge of burning the city, as of 'hating the human race.' In their very deaths they were made the subjects of sport; for they were covered with the hides of wild beasts, and worried to death by dogs, or nailed to crosses, or set fire to, and when the day waned, they were burned to serve for the evening lights. Nero offered his own garden-players for the spectacle, and indiscriminately mingled with the people in the dress of a charioteer.

—*From the* Annuals *of Tacitus. This passage testifies that only thirty years after Jesus' death, the historian Tacitus, takes the fact of the historical existence of Jesus and his crucifixion as a matter of course.*

PAUL

Paul, the apostle, who before was called Saul, after his great travail and unspeakable labors in promoting the Gospel of Christ, suffered also in this first persecution under Nero. Abdias, declareth that under his execution Nero sent two of his esquired, Ferega and Parthemius, to bring him word of his death. They, coming to Paul instructing the people, desired him to pray for them, that they might believe; who told them that shortly after they should believe and be baptized at His sepulcher. This done, the soldiers came and led him out of the city to the place of execution, where he, after his prayers made, gave his neck to the sword."

—*John Fox's Book of Martyrs*

PETER

Among many other saints, the blessed apostle Peter was condemned to death, and crucified, as some do write, at Rome; albeit some others, and not without cause, do doubt thereof. Hegesippus saith that Nero sought matter against Peter to put him to death; which, when the people perceived, they entreated Peter with much ado that he would fly the city. Peter, through their importunity at length persuaded, prepared himself to avoid. But, coming to the gate, he saw the Lord Jesus Christ come to meet him, to whom he, worshipping, said, "Lord, whither dost Thou go?" To whom He answered and said, "I am come again to be crucified." By this, Peter, perceiving his suffering to be understood, returned into the city, Jerome saith that he was crucified, his head being down and his feet upward, himself so requiring, because he was (he said) unworthy to be crucified after the same form and manner as the Lord was."

—*John Fox's Book of Martyrs*

ROME BURNS, NERO PERSECUTES CHRISTIANS
Test

1. In what year did Rome burn and Nero begin to persecute Christians?

   _____

   _____

2. How old was Nero when he came to rule Rome?

   _____

   _____

3. Up until the time of Nero how was Christianity viewed?

   _____

   _____

4. What did Nero think about Christians?

   _____

   _____

5. Who was first accused of setting the fires in Rome?

   _____

   _____

6. When the Christians were accused of setting the fires in Rome what did this lead to?

   _____

   _____

   _____

7. Why was Nero considered the worst persecutor of Christians in history?

   _____

   _____

   _____

8. What two apostles may have been executed during this time?

_____

_____

9. What eventually happened to Nero?

_____

_____

Review

1. What is a parable?

_____

_____

2. Who was John the Baptist?

_____

_____

3. Who was sent to tell Mary that she would be the mother of Jesus?

_____

_____

4. What was the "Pax Romana?"

_____

_____

5. In chronological order list all the events studied to date.

   Next to each place the approximate date.

DESTRUCTION OF JERUSALEM
Worksheet

1. What was the date of the destruction of Jerusalem?

   _____

   _____

2. When the Jews finally rebelled against Roman rule what did they say they would not do?

   _____

   _____

3. Who was Titus?

   _____

   _____

4. What did the Jews do during the nights and days?

   _____

   _____

5. What finally happened that caused the destruction of Jerusalem?

   _____

   _____

6. What did the Romans build to celebrate their victory?

   _____

   _____

7. What do many say about this event?

   _____

   _____

   _____

   _____

DESTRUCTION OF JERUSALEM
Project

News Report

Have the students write a news report about the destruction of Jerusalem. Then have them create an on-screen icon (like that shown below) that can be used while videotaping them giving their report imitating a news anchor just receiving this hot story off the satellite. Or have them work in groups and each takes a different role (news anchor, field reporter, and eyewitness).

DESTRUCTION OF JERUSALEM
Test

1. In what year did the Destruction of Jerusalem occur?

   _____

   _____

2. When the Jews finally rebelled against Roman rule, what did they refuse to do?

   _____

   _____

3. Who did Vespasian, the emperor, send to end the rebellion?

   _____

   _____

4. Describe how the Jews fought to defend Jerusalem. What finally occurred?

   _____

   _____

   _____

5. What does the arch in the Roman Forum represent?

   _____

   _____

   _____

6. What do some believe the Destruction of Jerusalem represents?

   _____

   _____

Review

1. How did the Persian Wars begin?

   _____

   _____

2. What is the legend about the founding of Rome?

    _____

    _____

3. Who were the first citizens of Rome?

    _____

    _____

4. Who were permitted to participate in the Olympic games?

    _____

    _____

5. In chronological order list all the events studied to date.

    Next to each place the approximate date.

    _____

    _____

    _____

    _____

    _____

    _____

    _____

    _____

    _____

    _____

POMPEII BURNS
Worksheet

1. In what year did Pompeii Burn?

   _____

   _____

2. What was Pompeii?

   _____

   _____

3. Who was emperor of Rome when Pompeii burned?

   _____

4. What does Mount Vesuvius have to do with the burning of Pompeii?

   _____

   _____

5. How many people were killed when Pompeii burned?

   _____

   _____

6. How long was Pompeii buried?

   _____

7. Why was Pompeii well preserved?

   _____

   _____

8. Why was the discovery of Pompeii important?

   _____

   _____

   _____

POMPEII BURNS
Project

Newspaper Article

Using the resources on the card use the sheet on the following page to write a newspaper article about the burning of Pompeii.

ROMAN ⬭ TIMES

Pompeii Burns!!

POMPEII BURNS
Project 2—Literature Unit

Pompeii... Buried Alive

Pompeii... Buried Alive is an easy to read book that will help you understand what happened to Pompeii when Mount Vesuvius erupted.

CHAPTER ONE

The Sleeping Giant

1. Fill in the blanks below.

What is the name of the mountain?

_____

What is the name of the town?

_____

2. Did the people in the town realize they were in danger?

_____

_____

3. Describe a volcano.

_____

_____

_____

_____

_____

_____

_____

POMPEII BURNS
Project 2, Page 2—Literature Unit

4. Describe a typical day in the city of Pompeii.

_____

_____

_____

_____

_____

_____

CHAPTER TWO

The Giant Wakes Up

1. What occurred when the top of Vesuvius blew off?

_____

_____

_____

_____

_____

_____

_____

_____

_____

_____

_____

_____

2. Draw a picture on the next page of the lava flowing from Vesuvius into Pompeii.

3. Who was the boy who witnessed the darkness over Pompeii from across the bay?

_____

_____

CHAPTER THREE

Buried Alive

1. What did the survivors who fled Pompeii find when they returned?

_____

_____

_____

POMPEII BURNS
Project 2, Page 4—Literature Unit

2. When the little boy Plinee grew up and became a writer, what did he write about?

    _____

    _____

3. After hundreds of years grass began to cover up the town of Pompeii.

    What happened to the town?

    _____

    _____

    _____

4. What occurred when people began to read Plinee's letters?

    _____

    _____

5. How was the buried city of Pompeii discovered?

    _____

    _____

    _____

    _____

6. What did the scientists discover?

    _____

    _____

7. In what country is Pompeii?

    _____

8. What is Pompeii like today?

    _____

    _____

POMPEII BURNS
Project 2, Page 5—Literature Unit

Pompeii... Buried Alive
Answers

Chapter 1
1. Vesuvius
   Pompeii
2. No
3. A volcano is a special kind of mountain which has a hole at the top. Deep inside it the rock is very hot and begins to melt. When this happens a gas is made. When the gas and rock mix together the gas pushes the melted rock out of the hole in the top of the mountain.
4. People would come to the city to sell their wares. Peddler and farmers brought food and shepherd's sheep. The families awoke and the slaves began a busy day of work. Children went to play. Many men headed to the bathhouse. By noon the town was full of people.

Chapter 2
1. The ground began to tremble and a huge cloud of dust and ash came pouring out of Vesuvius. People began to scream. They forgot about what they were doing. The cloud grew larger till it covered the sun causing darkness. Then tiny hot pebbles began to fall on the people in Pompeii. Everyone was running, pushing and shoving trying to get away. Some ran out of the town gates and others ran home or to the temple. Some chose to leave by way of the sea.

Finally people were unable to escape. The hot ashes began pouring out and they were trapped. The ashes spilled into the houses up to the second story windows. Finally a great cloud of poisonous gas rushed out of the mountain and covered Pompeii. Pompeii was gone.
2. Accept any reasonable picture.
3. Plinee

Chapter 3
1. They found the whole town had been buried alive.
2. Vesuvius the volcano that buried Pompeii.
3. People forgot that there was a city under the grassy fields. Eventually houses were built right above the buried town.
4. They began to question where Pompeii was. But no one knew.
5. One day some workers were digging and found pieces of an old wall, but they did not think much about it. A few years later digging again they found more buildings. One had the name Pompeii carved into it. Scientists began digging, they had found the buried city.
6. Beautiful gold bracelets, mosaics and people who had died.
7. Italy
9. It is like a great big museum without a roof. The most famous volcano in the world.

POMPEII BURNS
Project 3

Volcano Fun

Supplies
sand or dirt
1/2 cup water
empty soda can
quart bottle
4 tblspns soda
1/2 cup Elmer's glue
red food coloring
1/4 cup dishwashing liquid
1/4 cup vinegar
cookie sheet or shallow pan
funnel

Directions
1. Place the can in the middle of the cookie sheet
2. Mix sand, dirt, water and glue together. Mound around the soda can leaving the top open.
3. Using the matchboxes and cardboard, build small houses to place at the base of the volcano. After building the houses stick them into the sand.
4. Pour the baking soda into the can using the funnel.
5. Mix the water, dishwashing liquid, food coloring and vinegar. Pour into the quart bottle using the funnel.
6. Pour a little of the mixture into the crater.
7. The "lava" should erupt and flow over the crater down into the city.

Should the volcano not erupt, pour in a little more and use a metal stick to mix the ingredients in the soda can

POMPEII BURNS
Test

1. In what year did Popmpeii burn?

   _____

   _____

2. What was Pompeii?

   _____

   _____

3. Describe what occurred in Pompeii on August 24, 79 A. D.

   _____

   _____

   _____

4. How long did Pompeii remained buried?

   _____

   _____

5. Why was the discovery of Pompeii so important?

   _____

   _____

Review

1. Who were the Phoenicians?

   _____

   _____

2. Who participated in the original Olympics?

   _____

   _____

POMPEII BURNS
Test, Page 2

3. What is the legend of the founding of Rome?

_____

_____

_____

_____

4. Who wrote the Iliad and the Odyssey?

_____

_____

5. In chronological order list all the events studied to date.

   Next to each place the approximate date.

_____

_____

_____

_____

_____

_____

_____

_____

_____

_____

_____

_____

_____

SPLIT OF THE ROMAN EMPIRE
Worksheet

1. What was the date of the Split of the Roman Empire?

   _____

   _____

2. The Roman Empire had grown to _____ for one person to control. Why was this?

   _____

   _____

3. When Diocletian became emperor he split the empire into how many parts? Why?

   _____

   _____

   _____

4. Who was Maximian?

   _____

   _____

5. What did Diocletian declare about himself? What did he order everyone to do?

   _____

   _____

   _____

6. Why did civil war break out during this time?

   _____

7. Who was Constantine?

   _____

   _____

SPLIT OF THE ROMAN EMPIRE
Project

Color the sea *blue,* the Western Empire *orange* and the Eastern Empire *green* (see pg. 76 in *The Usborne Illustrated World History, The Romans*).

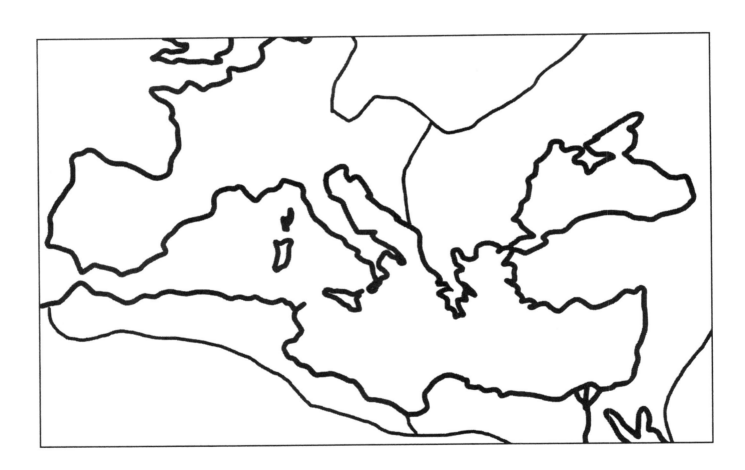

SPLIT OF THE ROMAN EMPIRE
Test

1. What was the date of the Split of the Roman Empire?

   _____

   _____

2. What was the problem with the major growth in the Roman Empire?

   _____

   _____

3. What did Diocletian do to take care of the growth in the Roman Empire?

   _____

   _____

   _____

4. Who was Maximian?

   _____

   _____

5. Describe Diocletian as an Emperor.

   _____

   _____

6. How did Constantine become a ruler of the Roman Empire?

   _____

   _____

   _____

SPLIT OF THE ROMAN EMPIRE
Test, Page 2

Review

1. What are the approximate dates of the Minoan culture?

   _____

   _____

2. What is the translation of the Greek word "phoinos?"

   _____

   _____

3. Why was Israel divided?

   _____

   _____

4. Who wrote the Iliad and the Odyssey?

   _____

   _____

5. In chronological order list all the events studied to date.

   Next to each place the approximate date.

   _____

   _____

   _____

   _____

   _____

   _____

   _____

   _____

CONSTANTINE AND THE EDICT OF MILAN
Worksheet

1. What is the date for Constantine and the Edict of Milan?

   _____

   _____

2. Legend has it that while Constantine battled for the empire, he had a vision of a flaming _____ in the sky and heard a voice saying "_____."

3. In Constantine's dream what sign was he told to put on his soldier's shields?

   _____

   _____

4. After Constantine won the war, what happened to him personally?

   _____

   _____

5. What was the Edict of Milan?

   _____

   _____

   _____

6. The Edict of Milan was the transition to the era of the "_____."

Constantine and the Edict of Milan
Project

Flag
Supplies

light blue construction paper
cotton balls
paint or markers

Directions
1. Glue cotton balls onto the construction paper to form a cross of "clouds" in the sky
2. Write or paint the English and Latin phrases on either side.

In Hoc Signo Vinces

In This Sign Thou Shalt Conquer

Constantine and the Edict of Milan
Project 2

The Edict of Milan (313 A. D.)

When I, Constantine Augustus, as well as I Licinius Augustus fortunately met near Mediolanurn (Milan), and were considering everything that pertained to the public welfare and security, we thought—, among other things which we saw would be for the good of many, those regulations pertaining to the reverence of the Divinity ought certainly to be made first, so that we might grant to the Christians and others full authority to observe that religion which each preferred; whence any Divinity whatsoever in the seat of the heavens may be propitious and kindly disposed to us and all who are placed under our rule And thus by this wholesome counsel and most upright provision we thought to arrange that no one whatsoever should be denied the opportunity to give his heart to the observance of the Christian religion, of that religion which he should think best for himself, so that the Supreme Deity, to whose worship we freely yield our hearts) may show in all things His usual favor and benevolence. Therefore, your Worship should know that it has pleased us to remove all conditions whatsoever, which were in the rescripts formerly given to you officially, concerning the Christians and now any one of these who wishes to observe Christian religion may do so freely and openly, without molestation. We thought it fit to commend these things most fully to your care that you may know that we have given to those Christians free and unrestricted opportunity of religious worship. When you see that this has been granted to them by us, your Worship will know that we have also conceded to other religions the right of open and free observance of their worship for the sake of the peace of our times, that each one may have the free opportunity to worship as he pleases ; this regulation is made we that we may not seem to detract from any dignity or any religion.

Moreover, in the case of the Christians especially we esteemed it best to order that if it happens anyone heretofore has bought from our treasury from anyone whatsoever, those places where they were previously accustomed to assemble, concerning which a certain decree had been made and a letter sent to you officially, the same shall be restored to the Christians without payment or any claim of recompense and without any kind of fraud or deception, Those, moreover, who have obtained the same by gift, are likewise to return them at once to the Christians. Besides, both those who have purchased and those who have secured them by gift, are to appeal to the vicar if they seek any recompense from our bounty, that they may be cared for through our clemency,. All this property ought to be delivered at once to the community of the Christians through your intercession, and without delay. And since these Christians are known to have possessed not only those places in which they were accustomed to assemble, but also other property, namely the churches, belonging to them as a corporation and not as individuals, all these things which we have included under the above law, you will order to be restored, without any hesitation or controversy at all, to these Christians, that is to say to the corporations and their conventicles: providing, of course, that the above arrangements be followed so that those who return the same without payment, as we have said, may hope for an indemnity from our bounty. In all these circumstances you ought to tender your most efficacious intervention to the community of the Christians, that our command may be carried into effect as quickly as possible, whereby, moreover, through our clemency, public order may be secured. Let this be done so that, as we have said above, Divine favor towards us, which, under the most important circumstances we have already experienced, may, for all time, preserve and prosper our successes together with the good of the state. Moreover, in order that the statement of this decree of our good will may come to the notice of all, this rescript, published by your decree, shall be announced everywhere and brought to the knowledge of all, so that the decree of this, our benevolence, cannot be concealed.

CONSTANTINE AND THE EDICT OF MILAN
Test

1. What is the date for Constantine and the Edict of Milan?

   _____

   _____

2. Describe the legend of Constantine.

   _____

   _____

   _____

   _____

   _____

3. What was one of the first acts of Constantine after his conversion?

   _____

   _____

4. What finally ended the persecution of Christians?

   _____

   _____

5. The transition to the era of the "_____" had begun.

Review

1. What do the seven hills have to do with the beginning of Rome?

   _____

   _____

2. What were basilicas?

   _____

   _____

3. Who was Alexander the Great's father?

_____

_____

4. Who was the famous student of Socrates? What kind of school did he start?

_____

_____

_____

_____

5. In chronological order list all the events studied to date.

   Next to each place the approximate date.

_____

_____

_____

_____

_____

_____

_____

_____

_____

_____

_____

_____

_____

_____

THE FIRST COUNCIL OF NICEA
Worksheet

1. What is the date given for the First Council of Nicea?

   _____

   _____

2. Why did Constantine summon 300 Christian bishops and deacons to meet on July 4, 325?

   _____

   _____

3. Where did these 300 bishops and deacons meet?

   _____

   _____

4. What is Arianism?

   _____

   _____

5. What was the result of the council?

   _____

   _____

6. To What important document did the summary of the council lead?

   _____

   _____

7. What are the three main points of the document?

   _____

   _____

   _____

   _____

   _____

THE FIRST COUNCIL OF NICEA
Project

Christian Banner

Supplies
12' wooden dowel
fabric paint
paint brushes
1'x2' piece of fabric
glue
1 1/2' of decorative cord

Directions
1. Copy the symbols at the bottom of this sheet onto a transparency then shine onto the wall
2. Tape fabric onto wall and trace the shape lightly in pencil onto the fabric
3. Paint the shape and letter the banner using fabric paint
4. Glue dowel to top edge then tie cord to either end

WE BELIEVE IN ONE GOD

FATHER, SON AND HOLY SPIRIT

SYMBOLS OF THE HOLY TRINITY

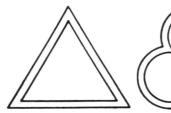   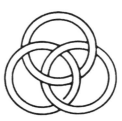 

EQUILATERAL TRIANGLE   TREFOIL   TRIQUETRA   THREE INTERLOCKING CIRCLES   FLEUR-DE-LIS

THE FIRST COUNCIL OF NICEA
Test

1. What is the date given for the First Council of Nicea?

   _____

   _____

2. Who summoned 300 Christian bishops and deacons to meet on July 4, 325 at the Imperial Palace in Nicea?

   _____

   _____

3. Why were the 300 bishops and deacons summoned?

   _____

   _____

4. What is Arianism?

   _____

   _____

5. What is the Nicean Creed and how did it evolve?

   _____

   _____

6. What are the three matters that the Nicene Creed settled?

   1. _____

   _____

   2. _____

   _____

   3. _____

   _____

Review

1. Who was Jeroboam?

   _____

   _____

2. What physical problems did Homer have?

   _____

   _____

3. Who were the Etruscans?

   _____

   _____

4. How did the colonization of Greece begin?

   _____

   _____

5. In chronological order list all the events studied to date.
   Next to each place the approximate date.

   _____

   _____

   _____

   _____

   _____

   _____

   _____

   _____

   _____

END OF THE WESTERN ROMAN EMPIRE
Worksheet

1. What is the date given for the End of the Western Roman Empire?

   _____

   _____

2. Who was constantly attacking the Roman Empire?

   _____

   _____

3. Most attacks were leveled against the _____ part.

4. List three barbarian tribes who invaded the Roman Empire.

   1. _____

   2. _____

   3. _____

5. Why were the attacks against the Roman Empire successful?

   _____

   _____

6. In 455, the _____ invaded Rome and destroyed it?

7. Who was Romulus Augustulus?

   _____

   _____

8. Who was Odoacer?

   _____

   _____

9. With what did the fall Roman Empire begin?

   _____

   _____

10. The Western Roman Empire was gone, but its influence on us will never _____.

END OF THE WESTERN ROMAN EMPIRE
Project—Modern Day Counterpart

The Greco-Roman period has given us other things besides Roman numerals and the Olympics. Draw modern day counterparts from the illustrated developments of Greece and Rome shown below.

Roman military highway

Ruins of Roman Baths at Bath, England

Greco-Roman architecture

Roman Bridge and Aqueduct at Nimes, France

END OF THE WESTERN ROMAN EMPIRE
Test

1. What is the date given for the End of the Western Roman Empire?

   _____

   _____

2. The _____ was constantly attacking the Roman Empire

   including Rome itself.

3. Against which part of the Roman Empire were most attacks leveled?

   _____

   _____

4. List three barbarian tribes who invaded the Roman Empire.

   1. _____

   2. _____

   3. _____

5. Why were the attacks against the Roman Empire successful?

   _____

   _____

6. In 455, who invaded Rome and destroyed it?

   _____

   _____

7. Who was the last emperor of the West?

   _____

   _____

8. In 476 a German captain named _____declared himself King

   of Italy and ruled from Ravenna.

9. What began the break up of the Empire into separate countries?

   _____

   _____

10. The Western Roman Empire was gone, but its _____ on us will never disappear.

Review

1. When Nero came to rule he no longer allowed Christians to worship God.

   Why did he do this?

   _____

   _____

2. How did Julius Caesar become Rome's ruler?

   _____

   _____

3. Who did the Romans destroy in the third Punic War?

   _____

   _____

4. What do the seven hills have to do with the beginning of Rome?

   _____

   _____

5. In chronological order list all the events studied to date. Next to each place the

   approximate date and Biblical reference if applicable.

   _____

   _____

   _____

   _____

CUMULATIVE REVIEW
Test

Card:

_____

_____

Date:

_____

TWO FACTS:

_____

_____

_____

_____

Card:

_____

Date:

_____

TWO FACTS:

_____

_____

_____

_____

_____

Card:

_____

_____

Date:

_____

TWO FACTS:

_____

_____

_____

_____

Card:

_____

Date:

_____

TWO FACTS:

_____

_____

_____

_____

_____

READING PROJECTS
Instructions

Teacher's Instructions for Integrating History and Writing

1. Vocab: Before giving the assignment the teacher should look at the vocabulary and make a judgement as to whether or not the students will be likely to know most of them. If the answer is yes, skip to step #2 and have them look up the vocabulary afterward. If not, have them look up the vocab words first.

2. Reading/Note-taking: have the students read the passage while taking notes using the "key-word method." In brief, this means **no more than 3** words from each sentence that will help the student remember what is said in it. Appropriate answers can, of course vary, but sample answers are given in the answer key. Two general rules can help these notes to be meaningful:
   a. Distilling the grammatical core—words that are part of the grammatical core of the sentence, particularly subjects, action verbs, direct objects, predicate nouns and adjectives.
   b. Note that *linking verbs* are not listed above. Though they are just as much a part of the grammatical core, they are easy to assume (i.e., instead of writing "Alexander was brutal," it is more effective to write, "Alexander brutal").

3. Title: have the students try to come up with a title for each paragraph. This forces them to try to look at each paragraph and try to understand its main point. Sample titles are given on the answer key.

4. Summary paragraph: Have the students turn the page and try to reconstruct, in brief, the essence of the original on a separate sheet of paper using only their notes.

5. Improved paragraph: have the students spruce up their paragraphs using a list of "modifiers", "power words" or grammatical constructions that can help the students to make their writing more interesting. (Andrew Pudewa's "Excellence in Writing" method is a good example of how to do this in practice.)

New Testament, Greece & Rome
Project—Example Grammar-History Sentences

Directions for History-Grammar Integration

We recommend the Shurley Grammar program as being the one which does the best job of teaching students the fundamental structure of the English sentence. Obviously, the sentences in the various sentences groups of Shurley are not all going to have any relationship with the content of their history, but we believe that making up extra practice sentences which have content culled from their history lessons can bring a beneficial "synergy" into the curriculum.

Several sentences derived from the content of the history lessons have been written and parsed as examples. Obviously, the possibilities are limitless.

It would also be worthwhile to have the children make up their own, history-related sentences. This could be done for the whole class to parse, or for their own, individual practice and improved sentences that are integral to the Shurley lessons.

```
                    SN     V        P  A  ADJ  OP   P  A  ADJ  OP
1. SN V       Homer wrote \ (about a golden age) (of the distant past). D
   P1
```

1. Homer wrote about a golden age of the distant past.
2. Who wrote about a golden age of the distant past? Homer/SN
3. What is being said about Homer? Homer wrote/V
4. About/P
5. About what? age/OP
6. What kind of age? golden/Adj
7. A/A
8. Of/P
9. Of What? past/OP
10. What kind of past? distant/Adj
11. The/A
12. SN V P1 check
13. (about a golden age), prepositional phrase
14. (of the distant past), prepositional phrase
15. Period, statement/D
16. Go back to the verb; divide the complete subject from the complete predicate.

NEW TESTAMENT, GREECE & ROME
Project—Example Grammar-History Sentences

```
                   SN     V-t    A      DO      P    PPA       ADJ    OP
2. SN V-t    Alexander/ destroyed the Persian Empire (with his powerful army).
   DO P2
```

1. Alexander destroyed the Persian Empire with his powerful army.
2. Who destroyed the Persian Empire with his powerful army?   Alexander/SN
3. What is being said about Alexander? Alexander destroyed/V
4. Destroyed what? Persian Empire/verify the noun
5. Does Persian Empire mean the same thing as Alexander? no/DO
6. Destroyed/V-t
7. The/A
8. With/P
9. With what? army/OP
10. What kind of army? powerful/Adj
11. Whose army? his/PPA
12. SN V-t DO P2 check.
13. (with his powerful army), prepositional phrase
14. Period, statement/D
15. Go back to the verb; divide the complete subject from the complete predicate.

```
                   SN     V-t PPA IO   A   ADJ      DO   IO
1. SN V-t    Socrates/ gave his audience a surprising oration!
   DO P3
```

1. Socrates gave his audience a surprising oration!
2. Who gave his audience a surprising oration? Socrates/SN
3. What is being said about Socrates? Socrates gave/V
4. Gave what? oration/verify the noun
5. Does oration mean the same thing as Socrates? no
6. Oration/DO
7. Gave/V-t
8. Gave oration to whom? audience/IO
9. What kind of oration? Surprising/Adj
10. A/A
11. Exclamation point, strong feeling/E
12. Go back to the verb; divide the complete subject from the complete predicate.

CHAPTER SUMMARY

Event:

Date:
Who
What

Where

NEW TESTAMENT, GREECE & ROME
Veritas Press History Song

This is the story of two great civilizations; one was Greece, the other was Rome.

Let's go back in history to 2200 B.C.
First came the Minoan culture.
2nd the Mycenean culture.
3rd the Trojan War between Sparta and Troy.
4th the Phoenician civilization. Thank goodness
    for their alphabet.
5th the division of the tribes of Israel resulted
    in two kingdoms.
6th came Homer and Greek Mythology.
7 the Greek Olympics.
8 came the founding of Rome in 753 B.C.
9 democracy began when Greece was
    colonized 750 B.C.
Then number 10 came the fall of Israel and Judah.
11 the prophets of God.
12 came the first republic of Rome,
    the people elected their rulers.
13 came the Persian Wars.
14 Pericles and the Peloponnesian War.
15 Greek Philosophers.
16 Nehemiah led the Jews return
    to Jerusalem.
17 came Alexander the Great.
18 the Architecture of Rome.
19 the rise of the Roman Empire, Greece
    had diminished while Rome increased.
20 the reign of Julius Caesar.
21 was Caesar Augustus.
22 the birth of Jesus Christ in the year 3 B.C.
23 was John the Baptist.
24 the Ministry of Christ.
25 the Crucifixion, Resurrection, and Ascension
    in 30 A.D.
Then 26 came the burning of Rome by Nero,
    wicked persecutor of Christians.
27 the destruction of Jerusalem in 70 A.D.
28 the burning of Pompeii.
29 the Roman Empire splits.
Then came number 30. Constantine and
    the Edict of Milan in 313 A.D.
Then 31 came the Council of Nicea 325 A.D.
32 the end of the Roman Empire 476 A.D.
Yes, then came the end of the Roman Empire 476 A.D.